SpringerBriefs in Applied Sciences and Technology

European Space Policy Institute

The books in this series cover various space-related domains including space policy and strategy, governance, space economy, space law and regulations, space diplomacy and international relations or space security among others. They aim at supporting a good understanding of the issue they cover and at providing ESPI perspectives on the topic. Each book explores an important area of space policy development and provides a comprehensive overview of the topic and an in-depth analysis of the main implications for the space sector. Information and positions provided in the reports are the result of a thorough background research including extensive literature review and key stakeholders interviews and of space policy experts analyses.

More information about this series at http://www.springer.com/series/15974

Clelia Iacomino

Commercial Space Exploration

Potential Contributions of Private Actors to Space Exploration Programmes

European Space Policy Institute

Springer

Clelia Iacomino
European Space Policy Institute
Vienna, Austria

ISSN 2191-530X ISSN 2191-5318 (electronic)
SpringerBriefs in Applied Sciences and Technology
ISSN 2523-8582 ISSN 2523-8590 (electronic)
SpringerBriefs from the European Space Policy Institute
ISBN 978-3-030-15750-0 ISBN 978-3-030-15751-7 (eBook)
https://doi.org/10.1007/978-3-030-15751-7

This Springer imprint is published by the registered company Springer Nature Switzerland AG
The registered company address is: Gewerbestrasse 11, 6330 Cham, Switzerland

Acknowledgements

The author is grateful to the people who have supported the research. Sincere thanks are extended to Jean-Jacques Tortora, Director of ESPI, and Sebastien Moranta, Coordinator of ESPI studies, who provided useful guidance and assistance during the research process.

Many thanks are also extended to Maria Cristina Falvella, Head of Strategies and Industrial Policy at ASI, for her precious support as well as to Silvia Ciccarelli, Research Fellow at ASI, for her suggestions and review. A special mention goes to Gabriella Arrigo, Head of International Relations at ASI, who was instrumental to initiate the project.

The author is also grateful to the entire ESPI staff for their support and help during the project. Genuine thanks are in particular offered to Stefano Ferretti, ESA Space Policy Officer; Alessandra Vernile, Project Officer at Eurisy; and Clémentine Decoopman, Executive Director at Space Generation Advisory Council, for their help.

Contents

About the Author

Clelia Iacomino is working as Resident Fellow at the European Space Policy Institute (ESPI) in Vienna, Austria, under a fellowship from the Italian Space Agency (ASI) and the Italian Society for International Organization (SIOI).

Previously, she worked as Analyst at Thales Alenia Space at the Strategic Business Intelligence Department in Rome. She holds an MA in international relations from La Sapienza University and a Master of Advanced Studies in space policy at SIOI-ASI-CNR, Rome.

Acronyms

AES	Advanced Exploration Systems Division
ASI	Italian Space Agency
ASTP	Apollo–Soyuz Test Project
BAA	Broad Agency Announcements
BIC	Business Incubation Centres
C3PO	Commercial Crew and Cargo Program
CAPEX	Capital Expenditures
CASIS	Center for the Advancement of Science in Space
CATALYST	Lunar Cargo Transportation and Landing
CCDev	Commercial Crew Development
CCP	Commercial Crew Program
CFI	Call for Ideas
CLEP	Chinese Lunar Exploration Project
CMSA	China Manned Space Agency
CNES	Centre National d'Etudes Spatiales
CNSA	China National Space Administration
CoECI	Center of Excellence for Collaborative Innovation
COF	Columbus Orbital Facility
COPUOS	Committee on the Peaceful Uses of Outer Space
COTS	Commercial Orbital Transportation Services
CRS	Commercial Resupply Services
CSOC	Common Operation Costs
CSS	Chinese Space Station
DLR	German Aerospace Center
DSG	Deep Space Gateway
DST	Deep Space Transport
E3P	European Exploration Envelope Programme
EF	Exposed Facility
ELIPS	European Programme for Life and Physical Science and Application in Space

EPC	Engineering, Procurement, and Construction
ER&T	Exploration Research & Technology
ESA	European Space Agency
ESPI	European Space Policy Institute
EU	European Union
ExPeRT	Exploration Preparation, Research, and Technology
FAA	Federal Aviation Administration
GER	Global Exploration Roadmap
GLXP	Google Lunar XPRIZE
HTV	H-II Transfer Vehicle
IAC	International Astronautical Congress
ICT	Information and Communications Technology
ILDD	Innovative Lunar Demonstrations Data
InSight	Interior Exploration using Seismic Investigations, Geodesy and Heat Transport
IPC	Industrial Policy Committee
ISECG	International Space Exploration Coordination Group
ISEF	International Space Exploration Forum
ISRO	Indian Space Research Organisation
ISRU	In-Situ Resource Utilization
JAXA	Japan Aerospace Exploration Agency
JKIC	Joerg Kreisel International Consultancy
LEAG	Lunar Exploration Analysis Group
LEO	Low Earth Orbit
LSP	Launch Services Program
MPLM	Multi-Purpose Logistics Modules
MPO	Mercury Planetary Orbiter
MSL	Mars Science Laboratory
NASA	National Aeronautics and Space Administration
NextSTEP	Next Space Technologies for Exploration Partnerships
NSC	National Space Council
NTL	NASA Tournament Lab
O&M	Observations and Measurements
OCST	Office of Commercial Space Transportation
OPEX	Operating and maintaining it
Orion CEV	Orion Crew Exploration Vehicle
OrionMPCV	Orion Multi-Purpose Crew Vehicle
PILOT	Precise and Intelligent Landing using On-board Technology
PM	Pressurized Module
PPP	Public–Private Partnership
PROSPECT	Platform for Resource Observation and in-Situ Prospecting for Exploration, Commercial exploitation and Transportation
PSC	Public Sector Comparator
PSLV	Polar Satellite Launch Vehicle
R&D	Research and Development

RI	Research Institutions
ROI	Return on Investment
Roscosmos	Russian Federal Space Agency
SAAs	Space Act Agreements
SciSpacE	Science in Space Environment
SLS	Space Launch System
SMEs	Small- and medium-sized enterprises
SNC	Sierra Nevada Corporation
SPACE	Spurring Private Aerospace Competitiveness and Entrepreneurship
SpaceX	Space Exploration Technologies Corporation
SPECTRUM	Space Exploration Communications Technology for Robustness and Usability between Missions
SPV	Special-Purpose Vehicle
SSA	Space Act Agreement
TTP	Technology Transfer Programme
UKSA	UK Space Agency
UN	United Nations
UNOOSA	United Nations Office for Outer Space Affairs
US	United States
USRR	Union of Soviet Socialist Republics
VC	Venture Capital
VfM	Value for Money

List of Interviews

Publicly available data and information were completed with the following experts' interviews:

- **Walter Cugno**, Vice President, Domain Exploration and Science at Thales Alenia Space.
- **Luca Del Monte**, Head of Industrial Policy and SME Division at European Space Agency.
- **Daniela Dobreva-Nielsen**, Business Development at AZO—Space of Innovation * Anwendungszentrum GmbH Oberpfaffenhofen.
- **Uli W. Fricke**, Managing Director at Triangle Venture Capital Group.
- **Laura Gatti**, Sales and Marketing Manager for ESA at Thales Alenia Space.
- **Gary Martin**, Senior Advisor Ministry of the Economy, Luxemburg.
- **Gabriele Mascetti**, Head of Human Spaceflight Department at ASI.
- **Luciano Saccani**, Senior Director, Business Development at Sierra Nevada Corporation's Space Systems.
- **Silvio Sandrone**, VP Advanced Projects and Products chez Airbus Defence and Space.

Chapter 1
Introduction

1.1 Background and Rationale for the Study

The global space activity, in particular in the field of outer space exploration and human spaceflight, two domains intrinsically related, has traditionally been driven by governments.

From a historical standpoint, the Cold War provided a particularly fertile geopolitical context for progress in these areas. Competition between the USA and the Union of Soviet Socialist Republics, trying to outdo each other's achievements, has given an incredible momentum to space exploration programmes. At the time, the large public budgets dedicated to space exploration were predominantly motivated by political and strategic objectives: on 12 September 1962, President John F. Kennedy proclaimed that the USA had chosen to forge the pathway to the Moon "not because it is easy, but because it is hard" [1] insisting that the USA would make efforts to explore outer space to demonstrate American greatness to the rest of the world.

After the success of the Apollo programme, the political incentive for space exploration weakened and public budgets for related programmes were substantially reduced. Yet, American space exploration ambitions were never officially scaled down, putting pressure on the National Aeronautics and Space Administration (NASA) to achieve comparable results with limited resources. In parallel, the USA and USSR entered a period of Détente symbolized, in the space exploration domain, by the Apollo–Soyuz Test Project (ASTP) in July 1975. This marked a change in the space race and the beginning of an era of international collaboration, as an alternative way to achieve challenging space exploration goals [2]. The emergence of other space-faring nations, in particular, Europe and Japan, expanded the possibility to achieve international partnerships. Among collaborations in the field of space exploration, the International Space Station (ISS), that President Ronald Reagan directed NASA to build in 1984, is the most ambitious and emblematic. The programme entered into force in 1998 with the signature of the Space Station Intergovernmental

C. Iacomino, *Commercial Space Exploration*,
SpringerBriefs from the European Space Policy Institute,
https://doi.org/10.1007/978-3-030-15751-7_1

Agreement (IGA) by 15 states and the launch of the first station module, Zarya, by Russia which joined the programme after decommissioning of the MIR station.

In parallel to the rise of international cooperation in space exploration, the Reagan administration also encouraged the emergence of commercial space with the concept of "new frontier" of economic development. This approach was also primarily motivated by the opportunity to conciliate American leadership and a reduction of government spending. Ever since, US space commercialization strategy intensified on an increasing number of space domains (i.e. space telecommunications, commercial space transportation, remote sensing…) through various governmental initiatives and the incremental adoption of a legal and regulatory framework to foster commercial endeavours. Space commercialization was not a preserve of the USA. In the late 70s, Europe had already engaged in this field with outstanding successes such as Arianespace, the first commercial space launch operator (1980) or SPOT Image, the first commercial dealer for space remote sensing (1982).

In this historical context, space exploration remained, however, and despite multiple attempts,[1] essentially funded and led by governments through national and international programmes. The substantial costs of space exploration missions and lack of business cases limited the emergence of commercial leadership in this field. As a consequence, and despite a strong political will, the involvement of commercial actors in space exploration programmes remained limited, in general, to the role of contractors.

This situation evolved to some extent with the retirement of the Space Shuttle and the introduction of the Commercial Orbital Transportation Services (COTS) programme. Driven by the objective to improve cost-effectiveness and share development and operations' risks with private partners, NASA implemented an innovative procurement scheme based on competitive, performance-based, fixed-price milestones [3]. Through the COTS and related Commercial Resupply Service (CRS) and Commercial Crew Program (CCP), NASA transferred a bigger share of responsibilities and risks to the private sector, focusing on the purchase of cargo and crew transportation services rather than vehicles. In this frame, the agency acted as an anchor customer, investor and advisor for the industry to stimulate private development of commercial space transportation systems [3]. These programmes marked an important milestone in the rise of commercial actors in the field of outer space exploration and human spaceflight and established a successful example for more ambitious partnerships between government and industry in this field.

Fostering the involvement of commercial actors in public programmes is nowadays a dominant consideration of governments and agencies who are increasingly eager to explore new mechanisms to take advantage of private contributions to engage in future programmes and achieve challenging space exploration goals. In general, various announcements and institution-led initiatives, such as the Calls for Ideas

[1] Note: These attempts were primarily related to the objective to use human spaceflight and space exploration systems for commercial purpose (e.g. use of the Space Shuttle as commercial orbiter and for in-orbit servicing, use of space stations for commercial purpose including technology developments or orbital tourism).

launched by the European Space Agency (ESA) to trigger a commercial utilization of the ISS, underline the increasing interest of space agencies in opening exploration programmes to commercial contributions and reap associated benefits.

The growing opportunity of a more prominent contribution of commercial actors to space exploration also lies in the so-called New Space ecosystem, a business-driven dynamic of the space sector which is characterized by the following interrelated trends:

- **New entrants** in the space sector including large information and information and communications technology (ICT) firms, start-ups and new business ventures,
- **Innovative industrial approaches** with announcements and initial developments of ambitious projects based on new processes,
- **Disruptive market solutions** providing, for example, integrated services, lower prices, reduced lead time, lower complexity or higher performance among other value proposition features,
- **Substantial private investments** from different sources and involving different funding mechanisms,
- **New industry verticals and space markets** targeting the provision of New Space applications.

In this new ecosystem, space exploration and human spaceflight have become domains of interest for private companies, entrepreneurs and investors, eager to engage in commercial endeavours and conduct business in these fields. Among new target markets pursued by commercial actors, space mining, orbital tourism or even planetary colonization were recently put under the spotlight by ambitious private project announcements.

This general context creates programmatic opportunities and strategic challenges for space agencies. For this reason, the European Space Policy Institute (ESPI) and the Italian Space Agency (ASI) decided to conduct a study on the *potential contributions of commercial actors to space exploration*. This study aims to investigate the current space exploration geopolitical, commercial and programmatic environment to identify elements that would drive, or prevent, a more prominent contribution of private actors to space exploration and to analyse the conditions, mechanisms and expected impacts/benefits of potential contributions.

1.2 Study Objectives and Scope

The general objective of the research is to analyse in depth the specific trends driving the increasing investment and involvement of private actors in the field of space exploration and characterize how this new dynamic can create new opportunities for agencies. Eventually, the study aims at providing European institutions involved in space exploration programmes with key takeaways on the evolving commercial ecosystem and insights on potential mechanisms to foster and implement successful contributions of commercial actors to achieve European strategic space exploration objectives.

More specifically, the study aimed to:

- Provide an overview of the global space exploration landscape including strategies, policies and programmes,
- Investigate the emergence and development of New Space trends in the field of space exploration including in particular:
  - the use of innovative public procurement instruments,
  - the entry of new actors, including entrepreneurs and non-space companies,
  - the emergence of disruptive business models addressing new potential markets,
  - the growth of private investment,
- Examine the potential benefits of a more ambitious contribution of private actors to space exploration endeavours,
- Assess the necessary conditions to achieve successful public–private partnerships.

The contribution of private actors to space exploration endeavours can be envisioned through two different angles:

- **Cooperative contribution**: Involvement of private actors in the frame of public programmes,
- **Independent contribution**: Creation and development of private endeavours in the field of space exploration independently from public programmes.

This research focuses on cooperative contribution, defined here as the mobilization of resources and/or capabilities of commercial actors to support the achievement of space exploration objectives in the frame of public programmes. The creation and development of private business ventures aiming at exploiting space exploration capabilities to address specific markets (e.g. asteroid mining) will be considered only to the extent that it creates new opportunities for public space exploration programmes (e.g. R&D and innovation, new services, convergence of missions). Therefore, and although independent private endeavours are mentioned in this report, the research focuses more thoroughly on the involvement of commercial actors in public space exploration programmes through, for example, public–private partnerships or provision of commercial services to support current and future missions. Public support mechanisms for private business development in the field of space (i.e. loans, subsidies, grants, legal framework) were excluded from the research.

For this study, information was collected on trends observed in different countries and regions with a more specific focus on the USA and Europe. Eventually, the author kept a European perspective on issues at stake and conclusions of this research are intended for a European audience primarily. Space exploration is defined here as the range of activities and missions aiming at extending human presence beyond Earth (i.e. including space stations occupation and operations) and at surveying, investigating, researching and/or exploiting outer space including in particular celestial bodies (asteroids, comets, planets and moons). This includes preparation, demonstration and operational missions and covers both human and robotic missions.

References

1. J.F. Kennedy, *Address at Rice University on Nation's Space Effort* (Rice University, Houston, Texas, NASA JSC, 1962)
2. D. Holland, *The American Space Exploration Narrative: Evolution of Space Exploration in the United States from the Cold War to Today* (University of Colorado, Denver, 2016)
3. National Aeronautics and Space Administration, *Commercial Orbital Transportation Services*. NASA (2014). Retrieved from https://www.nasa.gov/sites/default/files/files/SP-2014-617.pdf

Chapter 2
Global Space Exploration Landscape: Strategies and Programmes

2.1 European Space Exploration Strategy and Programmes

2.1.1 European Strategic Framework for Space Exploration

In Europe, space exploration, including human spaceflight and robotic exploration, has traditionally been handled by ESA in collaboration with national space agencies. The last official document presenting ESA strategy in space exploration was endorsed during ESA Council at Ministerial level held in Luxemburg on 2 December 2014. This document is the *Resolution on Europe's space exploration strategy* [1].

ESA strategy outlines the long-term planning for Europe's participation in space exploration, focusing on the next ten years but also taking into account the longer-term perspective. The document highlights that the current European Space Exploration strategy strongly relies on the ambitions, capabilities and commitments of ESA Member States as well as on opportunities offered by global cooperation with international partners. The priorities are to consolidate and reinforce the role of Europe as a key partner in international space exploration programmes and to maximize the socio-economic benefits of space exploration activities through, among others, the commercial valorization of related technologies and facilities for applications on Earth (such as life support, resources management, robotics and bioengineering) [1].

In line with the European priorities introduced above, ESA vision is based on four strategic goals highlighting the link between space exploration and its value for the economy and society:

- **Science**: strengthening European excellence in scientific research through opportunities for in situ investigations and the development of relevant instrumentation and enabling technologies,
- **Economics**: contributing to the competitiveness and growth of the European industrial sector by pushing the frontiers of knowledge and developing new technologies able to be applied in all fields on economic values,

C. Iacomino, *Commercial Space Exploration*,
SpringerBriefs from the European Space Policy Institute,
https://doi.org/10.1007/978-3-030-15751-7_2

- **Global Cooperation**: establishing a global cooperative framework to carry out several specific space exploration projects, involving in each case interested partners,
- **Inspirational Dimension**: attracting society, and in particular young generations to expand the limits of our knowledge, to the study of natural sciences and engineering, to the values of global cooperation in space and to the preparation of sustainable human presence in the solar system beyond Earth [1].

Regarding destinations to explore, ESA activities and planning focus on Low Earth Orbit (LEO) the Moon and Mars. These destinations are presented as part of a single exploration roadmap and ESA aims to maximize technology and system synergies among these different destinations [1]. These targets have been selected insofar because they allow ESA to pursue different objectives with the ultimate goal to land humans on the Moon and Mars within the next 20–30 years. These three destinations will allow Europe to (1) implement a variety of robotic and/or human missions to build a comprehensive set of capabilities for Europe, each mission building on the achievements of the previous ones, (2) make science progress on priority questions and (3) further build international partnerships.

Most ESA space exploration activities are implemented in the context of international cooperation and on the basis of complementarity and mutual benefits with a view to building long-term strategic partnerships with other space-faring nations [2]. This approach allows ESA to reach more ambitious achievements by benefiting from financial and technical resources of its partners, to develop and share technologies but also to position Europe as a key player in the global space exploration arena. ESA works with a range of international agencies with the objective to be positioned as a key partner, if not a critical one, in ambitious programmes and to find an appropriate role for European technology and science as well as opportunities to develop new capabilities. International cooperation also allows optimizing value for money by pooling resources, complementing each other's capabilities and sharing resulting benefits.

In this context, ESA has been an active and influential participant in the interagency coordination process within the International Space Exploration Coordination Group (ISECG), considering the work of this international forum as a component of its strategic planning process. Through its engagement in ISECG, ESA has supported the development of the Global Exploration Roadmap (GER) that was defined by ISECG in August 2013. In this occasion, ESA pushed for the inclusion of a single mission scenario that reflected a coordinated international effort to advance a consistent programme, enhanced through the availability of commercial services and use of public–private partnerships (PPPs). The ISECG and GER are presented in more details in Sect. 2.4.1.

Considering that cooperation is a key pillar of ESA engagement in space exploration, the agency, through its flexible LEO–Moon–Mars strategy, remains open to a variety of possible partnerships with other space agencies active in human spaceflight and robotic exploration as well as with commercial actors.

The European Union (EU), although increasingly involved in space, does not take an active part, at the moment, in the space exploration domain. This has, however, not always been the case, and the EU had actually envisioned such active participation in the past, right after the signature of the Lisbon Treaty in 2007 which gave to the EU a shared competence in space policy. The need for a European Space Exploration Programme is mentioned in a number of EU Council Resolutions in 2008 and 2009. Furthermore, the EU Council Resolution on *Taking forward the European Space Policy* adopted at the 5th Space Council in September 2008 identified Space Exploration as one of four new priority areas for the European Space Policy, underlining the importance of exploration in the context of European space activities [3].

In that frame, the first *EU-ESA International Conference on Human Space Exploration* was organized by the European Council and ESA in October 2009 in Prague. During this conference, Ministers from the 29 ESA and EU Member States met to prepare a roadmap leading to the definition of a common vision and strategic planning for space exploration [4]. During the event, ministers expressed their support for a major financial investment of the EU in space exploration.[1]

Following various developments in the intricate European space governance, the state of affairs has changed and space exploration is no longer considered a key priority for the EU. Remarkably, this domain was not mentioned in the Space Strategy for Europe adopted in October 2016 by the European Commission nor in the proposed regulation for the 2021–2027 Multiannual Financial Framework [5].

Figure 2.1 shows the evolution of key priorities and mentioned areas in successive EC documents [6]:

It is, however, important to note that the EU still supports several research activities related to space exploration through the Horizon 2020 R&D Programme. In 2014 and 2015 about EUR 30 million of funding was available from H2020 for R&D activities related to space exploration.[2] Noticeably the EU supports an H2020 Strategic Research Cluster on Space Robotics Technologies whose high-level roadmaps, prepared by the PERASPERA consortium (i.e. led by ESA) includes a planetary robotics track. End goals of the cluster include, for example:

- Martian Long-range Autonomous Scientist
- Martian Cliff Explorer
- Martian Crossover Explorer
- Lunar Crater Explorer
- Planetary Deep Driller

Such support could continue in the frame of Horizon Europe and other instruments that will be implemented as part of the EU Multiannual Financial Framework for 2021–2027.

[1]European Commission. *Final Report Summary—COFSEP (Analysis of cooperation opportunities for Europe in future space exploration programmes)*. Retrieved from European Commission: https://cordis.europa.eu/result/rcn/162462_de.html.

[2]European Commission. *Space Exploration*. Retrieved from European Commission: http://ec.europa.eu/growth/sectors/space/exploration_it.

European space policy topics	1988	1992	1996	2000	2003	2007	2011	2016
Space capacity foundation – upstream sector								
R&D activities	●	●	•	●	●	●	●	●
Launchers and launch services	•	●	●	●	●	●	•	●
Space industry	●	•	●	●	●	●	●	●
Space applications – downstream sector								
Telecommunications	●	●	●	●	●	●	●	●
Earth observation	●	●	●	●	●	●	●	●
Satellite navigation		•	●	●	●	●	●	●
Space science and exploration		●		●	●	●	●	
International cooperation		●	●	●	●	●	●	●
Defence and security								
Space for security issues		•	•	●	●	●	●	●
Defence and dual-use		•	●	●	●	●	●	●
Secured space infrastructures							●	●
Other aspects								
Training/careers in space sector activities	●		•		●	•		•
Financing the space sector			•		●	●		
Regulation for the space sector	●	•		•	●	●		•
Governance of European space sector	•	•	•	•	●	●	●	

Data source: Elaboration on European Commission documents. ● = key priority • = mentioned area

Fig. 2.1 European space policy priorities in Commission communications. *Source* European Commission [6]

2.1.2 *European Exploration Envelope Programme (E3P)*

In 2017, about 11% (633.0 M€) of ESA budget was allocated to human spaceflight and robotic exploration [7]. In response to the Resolution on Europe's Space Exploration Strategy adopted in Luxembourg in December 2014, it was proposed to consolidate exploration and human spaceflight activities in a single European Exploration Envelope Programme (E3P). The E3P was approved by the Council at Ministerial level at the end of 2016 in Lucerne and integrated the three ESA exploration destinations "as part of a single exploration process" [8].

The E3P is the main instrument to turn the goals and ambitions articulated in the ESA space exploration strategy into reality. The activities implemented under the E3P are the continuation of activities carried out under previous declarations, which remain active to cover the implementation of activities approved and funded prior to the entry in force of the E3P declaration. This includes:

- Declaration on European Participation in ISS Exploitation Programme,
- Declaration on the European Programme for Life and Physical Science and Application in Space (ELIPS),
- Declaration on the European Space Exploration Programme Aurore,
- ISS Exploitation Programme and additional declaration for a part of the European Transportation and Human Exploration Preparatory Activities Programme.

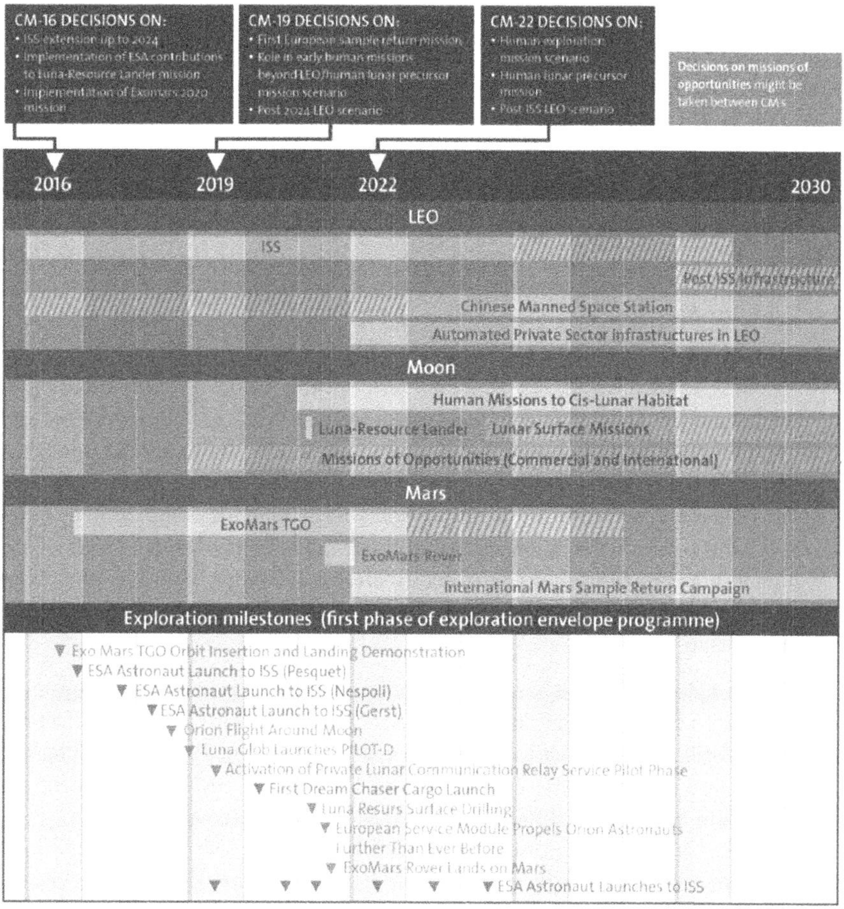

Fig. 2.2 European exploration envelope programme. *Source* ESA Exploration Roadmap

The overall E3P programme is structured in a series of steps, or periods, starting with a first transitional period covering 2017–2019. This transitional period is structured along seven main activities [8]:

- European participation in ISS Exploitation,
- Science in Space Environment (SciSpacE),
- Human Exploration beyond Low Earth Orbit,
- ExoMars,
- European contributions to the Luna Resource Lander Mission,
- Exploration Preparation, Research and Technology (ExPeRT),
- Commercial partnership.

Figure 2.2 presents the tentative planning of the E3P programme:

Ongoing ESA activities include:

- **European participation in ISS Exploitation:** As a result of ESA council in 2016, the agency "joined other ISS Partners in their objective to extend the duration of their involvement in ISS cooperation from the beginning of 2021 until the end of 2024" [9]. Extension beyond 2024 is currently discussed among partners, and no decision has been reached. ISS Exploitation activities can be divided into two distinct categories: ISS Core activities and ISS 2020 Barter elements.

  - ISS Core activities will secure the efficient operation of the Columbus module and of its payloads, in this way allowing the exploitation of the European LEO platform and the implementation of scientific and technology utilization activities. These technologies and tools should be developed also to allow astronauts to perform efficiently in deep space.
  - The development of Barter elements will allow ESA to discharge its obligations mainly for CSOC (Common System Operations Costs) and transportation requirements associated with the extension of the ISS Exploitation up to 2024. The activities to be carried out during the first period of the programme related to the main activity area of ISS Exploitation will include the completion of Orion ESM FM1 development, the assembly and manufacture of the second flight model of the ESM as part of the contribution to a Barter with NASA to cover partly ISS Common System Operations Costs and securing future astronaut missions in 2021–24.

  The main activities, to be carried out during the first period of the programme, in relation to ISS Exploitation, include ISS Operations until 2019 (a part of ISS Operations is still being covered by the ISS Exploitation Programme Phase2), infrastructure sustainability, competition of Orion ESM FM1 development and procurement and testing of the Orion ESM FM2 Barter element.
- **Science in Space Environment (SciSpacE)**: The objective of this programme is to support science activities and to deliver socio-economic benefits related to fundamental knowledge, contribution to global challenges, education and inspiration. The programme also aims to ensure the continuity of research in LEO for European science and finally to prepare scientific contributions for future Human Exploration of the solar system. Specific activities of this programme include science support activities, development of ISS experiment facilities, instruments and hardware and mission cost of non-ISS platforms (including ground-based facilities, Parabolic Flights, Sounding Rockets and ESA participation in an orbital capsule mission.
- **Human Exploration beyond Low Earth Orbit**: The Human Exploration beyond LEO aims to prepare potential contributions to international cooperative efforts for Human Exploration beyond LEO, securing a suitable role for Europe. The elements supporting Human Exploration beyond LEO will be limited in the first period of the programme to studies covering topics such as preparation of long-term ESM and preparation of investments in beyond LEO transportation, habitation and operations capabilities, which would be critical for future sustainable missions in cis-lunar space by European Astronauts.

Table 2.1 Current mapping of planned ESA contributions to Russian Mission *Source* ESA [11]

		Luna—Glob Lander	Luna—Resurs Orbiter	Luna—Resurs Lander	LPSR
Spectrum	Ground support	X	X	X	X
	Interspacecraft Link		X	X	X
Pilot	Landing sites characterization			X	X
				X	X
	Navigation for precision landing			X	X
Prospect	Drilling and sampling				X
	Sample processing and analysis				X
Other products	Major systems (to be determined)				X

- **ExoMars**: The objective of the ExoMars missions is to undertake world-class science (atmospheric science of Mars and astrobiology science on Mars) including in particular search for life (past or current). In addition, this programme would demonstrate key flight and in situ-enabling technologies for future exploration mission and provide telecom relay capability for later Mars missions. The activities to be carried out during the first period of the E3P are related to the ExoMars Trace Gas Orbiter (in orbit around Mars since October 2016) which will explore the atmosphere of Mars and provide a vital telecommunications relay capability for Mars missions of both ESA and other agencies. Furthermore, the programme will implement the ExoMars 2020 mission, including development, integration and testing of the European Mars Rover [10].
- **European contributions to the Luna Resource Lander Mission**: The provision by ESA of subsystems for the Russian robotic lunar programme, in particular for the Luna Resource Lander (Luna 27) mission has the objective to demonstrate European capabilities in view of future exploration missions, allowing access and exploitation of the lunar surface. The activities to be carried out during the first period of the E3P include the implementation of Precise and Intelligent Landing using Onboard Technology (PILOT), Platform for Resource Observation and in Situ Prospecting for Exploration, Commercial exploitation and Transportation (PROSPECT) and Space Exploration Communications Technology for Robustness and Usability between Missions (SPECTRUM) for various Russian lunar missions (Table 2.1) [11].

- **Exploration Preparation, Research and Technology (ExPeRT)**: The activities to be carried out during the first period of the E3P include the implementation of systems studies in the areas of Mars Sample Return, Phobos Sample Return, Post-ISS LEO utilization and lunar human and robotic exploration enabled by the Deep Space Habitat.
- **Commercial Partnerships**: The activities to be carried out during the first period of the E3O include the implementation of a series of ESA initiatives for soliciting and evaluating partnership opportunities (this central topic will be discussed in more details in the next chapter).

To conclude, the first period of the E3P addresses consistently the goals and objectives of ESA as presented in the strategy, including the three ESA target destinations: LEO, Moon and Mars. The programme aims at enabling midterm strategic exploration objectives: the continuation of user-driven research in Earth orbit and the demonstration of end-to-end capability for sample-return missions and Human Exploration of the Moon surface. The E3P programme responds to the considerations of ESA Member States, expressed in the Resolution on Europe's space exploration strategy, to have the three ESA exploration destinations viewed as "one strategy, one programme" [12].

European national space agencies play a central role in ESA exploration activities which are proposed as optional programmes but also support the European engagement in human spaceflight and space exploration with a number of complementary activities undertaken at the national level or in the frame of bilateral agreements with other space-faring nations.

For example, ASI plays an important role in the ISS program, not only through its significant participation to ESA programme for the development and use of the Columbus Orbital Facility (COF), a programme to which Italy contributed for 19%, but also thanks to its bilateral agreement with NASA. In this frame, ASI directly supplied NASA with three Multi-Purpose Logistics Modules (MPLM) which are pressurized cargo containers used for the shuttle cargo bay: Raffaello, Leonardo and Donatello.[3] Following this agreement, ASI has acquired rights of utilization equal to 0.85% of NASA resources and Italian astronaut flights. Negotiations with NASA have been established to further expand benefits for Italy in the field of human spaceflight and space exploration. ASI also recently signed an agreement with China Manned Space Agency (CMSA), including biomedical research and physiological experiments, on the consequences of long-duration space missions and on the technology needs for human spaceflight. Furthermore, this scientific collaboration can be helpful for the whole Italian R&D (Research and development) sector, combining Italian know-how and the availability of Chinese space infrastructures. Considering the relevant role that Italy has within ESA, this bilateral cooperation might pave the way to a full collaboration between ESA and CMSA of related manned space activities.

[3]Italian Space Agency. *The International Space Station (ISS)*. Retrieved from ASI: http://www.asi.it/en/activity/space-habitability/international-space-station-iss.

Other examples of complementary national activities include the recent agreement between the Centre National d'Etudes Spatiales (CNES) and the Indian Space Research Organisation (ISRO) in the field of future launchers and lunar exploration. It was in this context that CNES and the start-up Axiom Research Labs signed an agreement under which CNES will be taking part in the Team Indus mission to land a module and two rovers on the Moon in January 2018 [13]. CNES also signed a cooperation agreement with NASA covering the SuperCam instrument for the Mars 2020 rover [14]. The agreement followed-up the successful work of the two agencies, who had already pursued by them with the MAVEN project and the MSL (Mars Science Laboratory) mission's Curiosity rover. The last example is the decision made by DLR (German Aerospace Center) to directly finance a study to explore the possible use of the US spacecraft Dream Chaser being developed by the US Sierra Nevada Corporation (SNC) [15].

2.2 U.S. Space Exploration Strategy and Programmes

2.2.1 U.S. Strategy for Space Exploration

The USA have long been a leader and a pioneer in the effort to explore space and celestial bodies both through robotic exploration and human spaceflight with outstanding successes in these fields. Notwithstanding, recent years have been marked by a decline of US leadership as a result of indecisiveness for space exploration strategy and reduced political support. This decline was recently acknowledged by the re-established National Space Council (NSC) who called for a revitalization of American leadership in space and in particular in the field of space exploration.

When President Obama took office in January 2009, NASA was working to get astronauts to the moon by 2020, as part of George W. Bush's Constellation programme. Announced in 2005, the Constellation programme envisioned using the moon as a stepping stone to Mars and led to the retirement of the Space Shuttle fleet that would be replaced by new capsule-based cargo and crew transportation private services [16]. To achieve deep space exploration objectives, the programme also initiated the development of adapted launchers, Ares I and V, and of a new capsule designed to carry astronauts beyond Low Earth Orbit, the Orion Crew Exploration Vehicle (Orion CEV) [17]. In May 2009, the Obama administration ordered an independent review of the agency's human spaceflight plans, which came to be known as the Augustine Commission. The Commission's final report deemed Constellation to be significantly over budget and behind schedule. As a result, in 2010, President Obama cancelled the five-year-old programme, instructing NASA to instead get astronauts to a near-Earth asteroid by 2025, and then to the vicinity of Mars by the mid-2030s. Building on developments initiated by the Constellation programme, US Congress mandated the development of the Orion Multi-Purpose Crew Vehicle (Orion MPCV) and of the super-heavy-lift Space Launch System (SLS).

The US space exploration strategy marked again a turn from Obama administration's "LEO–Asteroid–Mars" path to come back to the former "LEO–Moon–Mars" Constellation programme with the signature NASA's Transition Authorization Act 2017 on March 25 by US President Donald Trump. The new law directed NASA to review its deep space exploration effort and confirmed the ultimate objective of a manned mission to Mars but using cis-lunar orbit as a first step on the journey and in particular to use the Moon as a test bed for research, development and demonstration of critical technologies, operations and infrastructure required for a manned Mars mission.

The US plans to return to the Moon were officialized during the first meeting of the reconstituted NSC on 5 October 2017. The council, which was disbanded in 1993, brings together senior federal officials to coordinate the US space policy under the chairmanship of US Vice President Mike Pence [18]. During the meeting Mike Pence declared that "*we will return American astronauts to the moon, not only to leave behind footprints and flags, but to build the foundation we need to send Americans to Mars and beyond (…) the moon will be a stepping-stone, a training ground, a venue to strengthen our commercial and international partnerships as we refocus America's space program toward human space exploration*" [19]. To put this speech into action President Trump signed the Space Policy Directive-1 which called NASA administrator to refocus America's space programme on Human Exploration and discovery and to "lead an innovative and sustainable programme of exploration with commercial and international partners to enable human expansion across the solar system and to bring back to Earth new knowledge and opportunities" [20].

Accordingly, the *NASA 2018 Strategic Plan* puts a strong emphasis on space exploration and capacity building in collaboration with commercial and international partners across the four strategic objectives of the agency presented in Fig. 2.3.

As part of Strategic Objective 2.2, the document underlines the plan of the agency to conduct Human Exploration in deep space, including to the surface of the Moon and more specifically to "extend human presence into cis-lunar space and the lunar surface, with capabilities that allow for sustained operations in deep space and the lunar surface" [21]. The document also emphasizes NASA intention to incorporate private sector innovation into NASA missions and programmes through partnerships that would allow the agency to "focus on new initiatives, improve the efficiency and effectiveness of the missions, and strengthen US global competitiveness" [21].

Although the general direction to be followed has been agreed at the highest political level and reflected in NASA Strategic Plan, the implementation remains, however, at a very early stage and major questions on funding and programme architecture have yet to be answered. To effectively return to the Moon, the USA will have to mobilize considerable resources which would substantially impact other programmes of the agency, including in particular the ISS. In this regard, NASA plans to "enable space-based Low Earth Orbit economy by transitioning ISS operations and maintenance to commercial and international partners" [21]. Accordingly, the budget of the US Government "proposes to end direct US Government funding for the space station by 2025 and provides $150 million to begin a programme that would encourage

NASA 2018 Strategic Plan Framework		
Theme	**Strategic Goal**	**Strategic Objective**
DISCOVER	EXPAND HUMAN KNOWLEDGE THROUGH NEW SCIENTIFIC DISCOVERIES.	1.1: Understand the Sun, Earth, Solar System, and Universe. 1.2: Understand Responses of Physical and Biological Systems to Spaceflight.
EXPLORE	EXTEND HUMAN PRESENCE DEEPER INTO SPACE AND TO THE MOON FOR SUSTAINABLE LONG-TERM EXPLORATION AND UTILIZATION.	2.1: Lay the Foundation for America to Maintain a Constant Human Presence in Low Earth Orbit Enabled by a Commercial Market. 2.2: Conduct Exploration in Deep Space, Including to the Surface of the Moon.
DEVELOP	ADDRESS NATIONAL CHALLENGES AND CATALYZE ECONOMIC GROWTH.	3.1: Develop and Transfer Revolutionary Technologies to Enable Exploration Capabilities for NASA and the Nation. 3.2: Transform Aviation Through Revolutionary Technology Research, Development, and Transfer. 3.3: Inspire and Engage the Public in Aeronautics, Space, and Science.
ENABLE	OPTIMIZE CAPABILITIES AND OPERATIONS.	4.1: Engage in Partnership Strategies. 4.2: Enable Space Access and Services. 4.3: Assure Safety and Mission Success. 4.4: Manage Human Capital. 4.5: Ensure Enterprise Protection. 4.6: Sustain Infrastructure Capabilities and Operations.

Fig. 2.3 NASA 2018 strategic plan framework [20]

commercial development of capabilities that NASA can use in its place" [22]. This proposal has, however, raised concerns in both political and technical spheres.

2.2.2 *NASA Space Exploration Programme*

NASA budget for space exploration represents an annual envelope of more than 8 B$ covering various activities including exploration systems development, scientific research, ISS operations and transportation among others (Table 2.2).

NASA new ambitions have yet to be fully reflected in programmatic documents defining in more details the architecture and roadmap of the implementation of NASA strategic goals. Notwithstanding, NASA has already worked on a general "LEO—Moon–Mars" programmatic framework and investigated different options.

In the report *NASA's Plans for Human Exploration beyond Low Orbit* published in April 2017, NASA has identified eight principles for a sustainable and affordable Mars crewed space programme. Among these principles, the agency plans to rely

Table 2.2 NASA fiscal year 2018 budget request [23]

Budget authority, dollars in millions	FY 2014 actual	FY 2015 actual	FY 2016 operation plan	FY 2017 enacted	FY 2018 budget request
Exploration	**3,417.2**	**3,542.7**	**3,996.2**	**4,324.0**	**3,934.1**
Exploration systems development	3,115.2	3,211.5	3,640.8	3,929.0	3,584.1
Exploration research and development	302.0	331.2	355.4	395.0	350.0
Space operations	**4,470.0**	**4,625.5**	**5,032.3**	**4,950.7**	**4,740.8**
Space Shuttle	–	7.7	5.4	–	0.0
International space station	1,566.8	1,524.8	1,436.4	–	1,490.6
Space transportation	2,093.3	2,254.0	2,667.8	–	2,415.1
Space and flight support	809.9	839.0	922.7	–	835.0

on "new international and commercial partnerships that leverage current ISS partnerships and build new cooperative ventures for exploration" [24, see also 25] and "uninterrupted expansion of human presence into the solar system by establishing a regular cadence of crewed missions to cis-lunar space" [24, see also 25].

NASA also outlined three general stages for the Journey to Mars: Earth Reliant, Proving Ground and Earth Independent. For each stage, there is the objective to create an incremental approach, proving the required capabilities and building the systems needed to complete each stage of the mission. NASA document "*human exploration and operations exploration objectives*" published in September 2016 [26] and further divides the human space exploration programme into five successive phases. Each phase is planned to end with a transition mission to demonstrate achievements and prepare the next phase.

- **Phase 0** encompasses current space exploration activities and aims to demonstrate a range of key capabilities, including commercial ones, using the ISS as a test bed,
- **Phase 1** consists in a set of demonstration missions using the SLS and Orion spacecraft (Exploration Mission 1 and 2—EM-1/EM-2) to prepare and eventually conduct, a crew mission in cis-lunar orbit,
- **Phase 2** would build on previous achievements to prepare a long-duration crew mission of at least one year,
- **Phase 3** is still undefined but would conclude with a crew mission in Mars orbit,
- **Phase 4**, as a final step, would conclude with a robotic and then crewed mission on Mars surface.

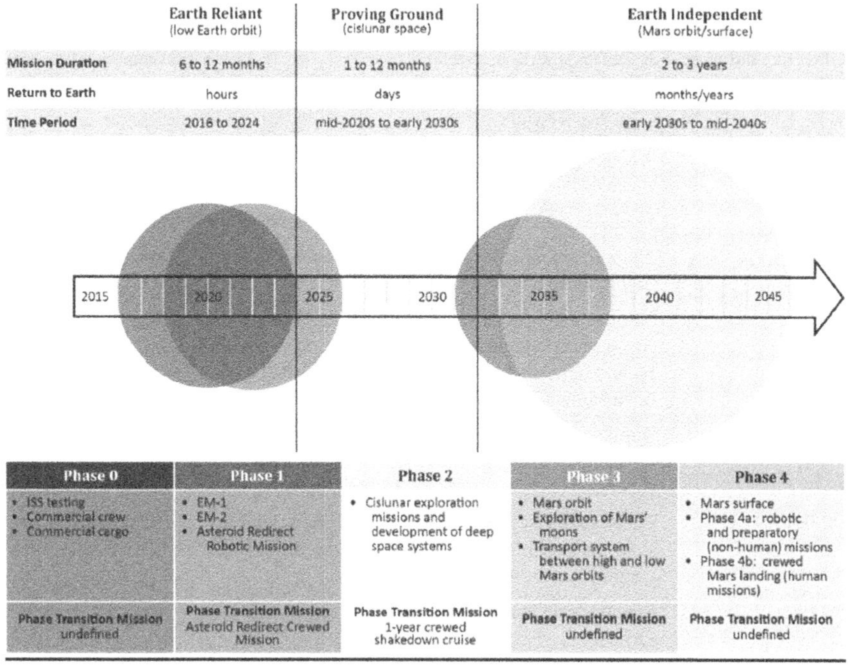

Fig. 2.4 Summary of NASA's plan for the journey to Mars [25]

Figure 2.4 provides an overview of the NASA plan including stages and phases described above.

2.2.2.1 Current Space Exploration Activities and ISS Operations

The agency uses the term Phase 0 to describe its current activities in LEO, in particular the testing of deep space subsystems on the ISS and the transportation of cargo and crew by the US companies. The ISS program is therefore at the core of Phase 0 (Table 2.3), which involves research and testing on the ISS with the aim to facilitate deep space, long-duration crewed missions.

As shown in Table 2.4, NASA expects to spend between \$3 and \$4 billion annually on ISS operations and maintenance through 2024.

The 2017 Transition Authorization Act also directed NASA to develop an "ISS transition plan" [27]. This plan solicits NASA to assess both its research on the ISS to support the agency's exploration objectives and to develop commercial activities in LEO. In addition, it requires cost estimates of extending ISS to 2028 and 2030. The Congress affirmed in this section that "an orderly transition for the US human spaceflight activities in Low Earth Orbit from the current regime that relies heavily

Table 2.3 Phase 0—objectives exploration systems testing on ISS and in Low Earth Orbit

Objective number	Requirement description	Objective category
P0-01	Acquire routine round-trip US crew transportation to Low Earth Orbit	Transportation
P0-02	Acquire routine US cargo transportation to Low Earth Orbit	Transportation
P0-03	Evaluate communications with increased delay	Working in space
P0-04	Demonstrate in-space exploration class extravehicular activity technologies	Working in space
P0-05	Demonstrate exploration environmental control and life support system and environmental monitoring technologies and validate real-time on-orbit environmental monitoring	Working in space
P0-06	Validate in-space fire detection, suppression, and clean-up technologies suitable for exploration missions	Working in space
P0-07	Demonstrate radiation monitoring technologies in Low Earth Orbit and evaluate radiation mitigation capabilities	Working in space
P0-08	Demonstrate autonomous operations in Low Earth Orbit	Working in space
P0-09	Demonstrate human and robotic mission operations	Working in space
P0-10	Evaluate technologies that may enable operations with reduced logistics capabilities	Working in space
P0-11	Demonstrate docking and close-proximity technologies and operations	Working in space
P0-12	Enable science community objectives in Low Earth Orbit	Working in space
P0-13	Demonstrate crew acclimation to and from zero gravity	Staying healthy
P0-14	Demonstrate medical diagnosis capability and treatment protocols for exploration missions	Staying healthy
P0-15	Demonstrate protocols to understand crew task performance and operations planning for human space missions	Staying healthy
P0-16	Demonstrate countermeasures to mitigate the hazards of long-duration spaceflight	Staying healthy
P0-17	Demonstrate long-duration viability and stability of food and pharmaceuticals	Staying healthy

Table 2.4 ISS budget based on FY18 president's budget request [27]

ISS budget	Average FY18-22 [25]
Total	$3.4B
O&M	$1.2B
Crew/cargo	$1.8B
Research	$0.4B
NL	$15M

on NASA sponsorship to a regime where NASA is one of many customers of a Low Earth Orbit commercial human spaceflight enterprise may be necessary" [28].

2.2.2.2 Next Phases

Next phases of the NASA space exploration programme will highly depend on the results of the current discussions about the continuation of ISS operations beyond 2024 and about the architecture of a cis-lunar programme including a Deep Space Gateway and Transport or alternative options [28].

As of today, Phase 1 is planned to involve exploration near the moon using technologies demonstrated during Phase 0 to allow the agency to gain experience with extended operations farther from Earth than previously completed. These missions will enable NASA to develop and demonstrate new techniques and apply innovative approaches to solving problems in preparation for longer-duration missions far from Earth.

NASA will test its new deep space exploration system beginning with an integrated, uncrewed flight of SLS and Orion, known as Exploration Mission-1. This flight test will be the first for the Orion spacecraft atop NASA's Space Launch System (SLS). Exploration Mission-1 will pave the way for following crewed missions, which will also assemble the Deep Space Gateway. The target launch date for Exploration Mission-1 is 2019 [25]. In addition to demonstrating the safe operation of the integrated SLS rocket and Orion spacecraft, the agency is also looking to build a crew-tended spaceport in lunar orbit within the first few missions that would serve as a gateway to deep space and the lunar surface. This Deep Space Gateway would have a power bus, a small habitat to extend crew time, docking capability, an airlock and serviced by logistics modules to enable research. The DSG concept includes a power and propulsion element, a small habitat and a logistics module for research. The three primary elements of the gateway, the power and propulsion bus and habitat module and a small logistics module(s) would take advantage of the cargo capacity of SLS and crewed deep space capability of Orion. The gateway will be developed, serviced and exploited in collaboration with commercial and international partners (Fig. 2.5).

Phase 2 will confirm NASA capabilities to perform long-duration human missions beyond the Moon. For those destinations farther into the solar system, including

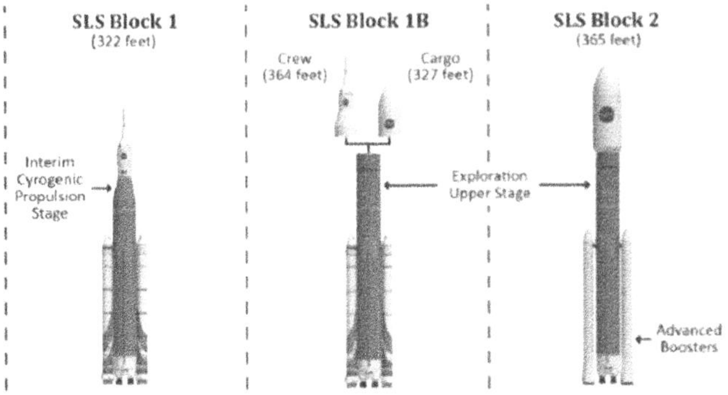

	SLS Block 1	SLS Block 1B	SLS Block 2
Scheduled completion date	2018	2021 to 2023	no earlier than 2028
Vehicles needed	1	approximately 7	unknown
Upgrades	n/a	Exploration Upper Stage	Advanced Boosters
Cargo payload fairing size (width by height)	n/a	8.4 meters by 27.4 meters	10 meters by 27.4 meters
Co-manifested payload for crew version	n/a	6 to 10 metric tons	10+ metric tons
Upmass to low Earth orbit	70 metric tons	105 metric tons	130 metric tons
Upmass to cislunar orbit	24 metric tons	40 metric tons	52 metric tons
Upmass to Mars	20 metric tons	33 metric tons	41 metric tons

Fig. 2.5 SLS versions for journey to Mars architecture. *Source* NASA [29]

Mars, NASA envisions a Deep Space Transport spacecraft. This spacecraft would be a reusable vehicle that uses electric and chemical propulsion and would be specifically designed for crewed missions to destinations such as Mars. The transport would take the crew out to their destination, return them back to the gateway, where it can be serviced and sent out again. The transport would take full advantage of the large volumes and mass that can be launched by the SLS rocket, as well as advanced exploration technologies being developed now and demonstrated on the ground and aboard the International Space Station [30]. This second phase will culminate at the end of the 2020s with a one-year crewed mission aboard the transport in the lunar vicinity to validate the readiness of the system to travel beyond the Earth–Moon system to Mars and other destinations and build confidence that long-duration, distant human missions can be safely conducted with independence from Earth. Through the efforts to build this deep space infrastructure, this phase will enable explorers to identify and pioneer innovative solutions to technical and human challenges discovered or engineered in deep space.

The gateway and transport could potentially support mission after mission as a hub of activity in deep space near the moon, representing multiple countries and agencies with partners from both government and private industry.

2.2.3 *Other NASA Space Exploration Missions*

Additional single missions are also planned or under development in the field of space exploration.

With the InSight programme (Interior Exploration using Seismic Investigations, Geodesy and Heat Transport), part of the NASA Discovery Programme, the agency aims to send a lander to Mars to study the deep interior and subsurface of Mars. The lander is planned for launch in 2018. The Mars 2020 rover will also complement NASA fleet of robots on the Red Planet to look for signs of past microbial life, gather samples for future return to Earth and investigate resources that could someday support astronauts [31]. The rover is planned for launch in 2020.

NASA's first asteroid sample-return mission, OSIRIS-Rex, will also arrive at the near-Earth asteroid Bennu in August 2018 and will return a sample for study in 2023. The mission will support scientist to explore how planets formed and how life began, as well as improve the understanding of asteroids that could impact Earth.

Finally, the Europa Clipper is a NASA's mission with the objective to investigate the habitability of Jupiter's icy moon Europa now has a formal name: Europa Clipper. The mission is being planned for launch in the 2020s, arriving in the Jupiter system after a journey of several years. The first mission plan mission plan includes 40–45 flybys, during which the spacecraft would image the moon's icy surface at high resolution and investigate its composition and the structure of its interior and icy shell. The ultimate aim of Europa Clipper is to determine if Europa is habitable, possessing all three of the ingredients necessary for life: liquid water, chemical ingredients and energy sources sufficient to enable biology.

2.3 Space Exploration in Other Countries and Agencies

2.3.1 *Russia*

Russia has also been a leader in space exploration and human spaceflight and has achieved a series of "first", including: the first human in space (Yuri Gagarin), the first unmanned lunar and Martian landings (Luna 1; Mars 3), the first space station (Salyut), the first spacewalk (cosmonaut Alexey Leonov on Voskhod 2), the first Moon impact (Luna 2), the first image of the far side of the moon (Luna 3) and unmanned lunar soft landing (Luna 9) or the first space rover (Lunokhod 1) among others. After the collapse of the Soviet empire, Russian progressively lost leadership in space but maintained critical competencies that are still core components of the global space exploration effort, in particular for human spaceflight activities [32].

Russia was a part of ISS construction from the beginning, and in 1998, the Zarya control module was the first element launched. In 2011 and 2015, across dozens of flights, the progress has experienced only a handful of failures over the space station's lifetime, providing regular crew transportation to the ISS. In 2013, the

Russian Federal Space Agency (Roscosmos) and NASA signed an agreement to continue using the Soyuz spacecraft and to send American astronauts to the ISS until 2017. Currently, the Russian position about the post-ISS is not clear. On the one hand, the agency stated that it would separate its ISS modules in 2024 to form the basis of a new Russian national space station but, during a recent speech at the 33rd Space Symposium in Colorado Springs, Igor Komarov, the head of Russia's Roscosmos space agency, affirmed that "Russia is open to staying until 2028" [33].

As for Mars Exploration, Russia is now looking to a major Mars mission. Most recently, the Phobos-Grunt, launched in cooperation with China to the Martian Moon Phobos, failed in 2012 when the probe could not break free of Earth's orbit. Actually, the agency is set to launch another probe Phobos-Grunt 2 to the Martian moon by 2022. Lately, Roscosmos and ESA have teamed up in the development of a joint ExoMars exploration programme. The first part was launched in 2016, placing a trace gas research and communication satellite into Mars orbit and releasing a stationary experimental lander. The second part is planned to land a rover in 2020 that would be able to drill the planet's soil.

Russia also has plans for robotic lunar missions, including a lander and a sample-return spacecraft. In 2015 the European and Russian space agencies announced plans to join forces to build a permanent human settlement on the Moon [32–34]. The venture, named Luna 27, is set to launch its first mission by the mid-2020s. In 2017, during 68th International Astronautical Congress (IAC), Roscosmos and NASA have agreed to cooperate on the NASA-led project to build the first lunar space station, part of a long-term project to explore deep space and send humans to Mars. The project envisages building a crew-tended spaceport in lunar orbit that would serve as a "gateway to deep space and the lunar surface" and as technology and operational test bed for future human missions to Mars [35].

2.3.2 China

China's space exploration strategy has identified robotic exploration of the Moon and manned spaceflight as the two important priorities. China's space exploration and human spaceflight's goals have been articulated in a series of 5-year White Papers, the last issued in December 2016. The programmes are divided into human spaceflight, robotic exploration of the Moon and other missions.

Regarding human spaceflight, the main attention is on the activities and technologies required for the future Chinese Space Station (CSS). The core module Tianhe-1 will be launched in 2018 and this will be followed by Tianzhou-2, a cargo and refuelling spacecraft which will dock and supply Tianhe-1 in LEO orbit, while the assembly of the station should be ready by 2022–24 [32].

Concerning robotic exploration, China became the third country, after Russia and the USA, to land a spacecraft on the lunar surface with the Chang'e-3 mission in late 2013. By the end of 2017, China National Space Administration (CNSA) is preparing to launch Chang'e-5, the country's first lunar sample-return mission, followed by Chang'e-4, the first spacecraft to attempt a landing on the lunar surface. The Chang'e-5 mission is the third and final step of the robotic Chinese Lunar Exploration Project (CLEP), but not only, will it set the stage for the alleged fourth phase of both CLEP and the HSF programme: a human footprint on the Moon. Indeed, in the long term, China has set ambitions for human lunar missions, although the timetable for those is uncertain [32].

Other relevant projects within the next five years include a new exploration mission to Mars, with the launch of a new Mars probe and lander by 2020 and a series of key space sciences missions within broader programmes such as the Sun–Earth Connection (SEC) programme and the Black Holes Probe (BHP) programme, which is intended to study high-energy processes of cosmic objects and black hole physics.

China is collaborating with the United Nations (UN) to arrange scientific experiments aboard that country's space station. The United Nations Office for Outer Space Affairs (UNOOSA) and China's Manned Space Agency have invited applications from UN Member States to conduct experiments on CSS. In 2016, the two signed a memorandum of understanding to work together to progress with the development of the space capabilities of UN member states via opportunities to use the station, which China expects to be operational by 2022 [36].

The year 2019 started with a new landmark achievement for China's space programme: the Chang'e-4 mission "lifted the mysterious veil" by accomplishing mankind's first soft landing on the far side of the Moon. The spacecraft, launched on 7 December 2018, landed on the south pole's Aitken basin, the deepest and oldest crater of the Moon, on 3 January 2019. Following the successful touchdown, the 140-kg *Yutu* rover was released from the lander. Both systems are now performing a series of scientific tasks, including measurements of the Moon chemical structure, astronomical observations as well as biological experiments to grow plants in the lunar environment for the first time.

The successful execution of the mission was hailed as a formidable feat for China from a geopolitical standpoint. This feat did not come as a surprise for the space community and marks the steady progress of Beijing's plans for lunar exploration. Chang'e-4 is actually part of an ambitious decade-long programme whose roots date back to the late 1980s. The programme, as officially approved by the Chinese Communist Party in 2003, is based on an incremental approach that aims to successively fulfil three major objectives: (1) orbiting around the Moon (Chang'e-1 in 2007 and Chang'e-2 in 2010); (2) landing and roving on the Moon (Chang'e-3 in 2013 and now Chang'e-4) and (3) returning lunar samples back to Earth. This last objective will be achieved with Chang'e-5 and 6 sample-return missions, which are scheduled for launch as early as 2019 and 2020, respectively.

This will mark the completion of the third stage of China's Lunar Exploration Programme (CLEP) and pave the way to more daunting exploration missions, including, most notably, a taikonaut's Moon landing. Indeed, thanks to the concomitant advancement of the Shenzhou/Tiangong human spaceflight programme, it is expected that China will have mastered all the building blocks required to enable such mission by the early 2020 s. The mission will, however, probably not be part of the next (2021–2025) Five-Year-Plan—which will likely focus on the assembly and exploitation of China's Space Station—and should be put off to the 2026–2030 Five-Year Plan. This likely stems from a technical and political cautiousness as well as from a willingness to consider more demanding plans to go beyond US achievements with the Apollo programme. The alleged prospect of constructing an outpost near the lunar south pole to enable extended stays for Chinese taikonauts as well as the landing of a real *Chang'e* (i.e. a female astronaut) would substantiate the differentiation with the USA and add to China's international prestige and leadership.

Irrespective of their specific configuration and implementation timeframes, Chinese lunar plans, together with the position of the USA on a renewed American leadership in space, raise a number of questions for the international space community and, more importantly, open the way for a new era of space exploration structured around a mix of cooperation and competition.

2.3.3 Japan

Japan is a partner in the ISS program and its participation in the ISS has two important elements: the exploitation of the Japanese experiment module KIBO (Hope) and the H-II Transfer Vehicle (HTV). Japan's HTV is an automated cargo spacecraft used to resupply the KIBO and the ISS and the KIBO module is the first manned experiment facility, and it is the largest experiment module on ISS. The KIBO consists of two experiment facilities, the Pressurized Module (PM) and the Exposed Facility (EF).

Japan is the first country to have successfully implemented an asteroid sample-return mission. The Hayabusa mission, launched in May 2003, explored the near-Earth asteroid Itokawa and successfully returned some samples to Earth in June 2010. The successor is Hayabusa2, which revealed several new technologies and returned to Earth in June 2010. Hayabusa2 was launched on 3 December 2014. It is scheduled to arrive at the C-type asteroid in mid-2018, staying around there for one and a half years before leaving the asteroid at the end of 2019 and returning to Earth around the end of 2020.

Currently, JAXA is involved in a joint mission with ESA, named BepiColombo, which is Europe's first mission to Mercury. The mission will set off in 2018 and consists of two orbiters. Mercury Planetary Orbiter (MPO) will observe the surface and interior; Mercury Magnetospheric Orbiter (MMO) will observe the magnetic field and the magnetosphere.

Regarding the Lunar Exploration Programme, the Japan Aerospace Exploration Agency (JAXA)'s first lunar landing is planned to be launched in 2018. The programme is named SLIM and aims to establish a method for pinpointing landings that would make it possible to approach a target area with a level of accuracy ranging in the hundreds of metres.

With the help of the USA, Japan is planning to land astronauts on the moon by 2030. The JAXA envisions the human missions to the moon to study and make use of water ice deposits at lunar poles. This strategic plan would "involve making use of NASA's proposed Deep Space Gateway in cis-lunar space, which would serve as the jumping-off point for expeditions to the lunar surface" [37].

Recently, on 24 January 2018, JAXA and NASA signed a joint statement, declaring their mutual interest in future cooperation in space exploration. The two space agencies agreed to recognize each other's space exploration activities, recognizing their committed partnership in all mission areas, such as human and robotic exploration, Earth and space science and especially through the ISS program.

The statement also mentioned future missions, as well as the Deep Space Gateway, a cis-lunar space station project initiated by NASA and involving ESA, Roscosmos, JAXA and the Canadian Space Agency (CSA). JAXA also agreed to recognize the Deep Space Gateway, along with NASA's Space Launch System and Orion spacecraft, as a fundamental step that can benefit from contributions and technological expertize from both agencies [38].

Finally, at ISEF help in Tokyo in 2018, and ESA announced a joint statement which included a proposed lunar demonstration mission tentatively known as Heracles. According to the statement, both agencies will begin a feasibility study of a possible human lunar demonstrator mission via the Lunar Orbital Platform-Gateway, a project that will include the CSA. The mission will be confirmed in 2019 if the study outcome is promising [39].

2.3.4 *India*

Space exploration and human spaceflight activities have been recently taken up also by the Indian Space Research Organisation (ISRO). Since the last decade, ISRO embarked on New Space endeavours that include lunar and Mars exploration, as well as technological development for autonomous human spaceflight.

Within the recently concluded 12th Five-Year Plan (2012–2017) ISRO has been more specifically working on the continuation of its Chandrayaan lunar mission and on the Mangalyaan Mars probe, which was launched on 5 November 2013, making India the first country to reach a Mars orbit in the first try. Currently, India is preparing for the launch of Chandrayaan-2, the follow-up lunar lander, whose launch is planned for 2018. Within the 12th Five-Year Plan, funds have been also allocated for the development of technologies and capabilities that are critical for human spaceflights, such as for instance a recovery capsule. It is expected that India will join the club of space-faring nations with autonomous manned flight capabilities in the next decade.

With regard to private initiatives in space exploration, Team Indus is the first private Indian aerospace start-up that won one milestone prize: the Landing Prize of the Google Lunar XPrize, for a total of $1 million in winnings. In 2016, the start-up late stipulated a contract with ISRO for a launch of its lander, which will also carry a rover from Team Hakuto of Japan, on a Polar Satellite Launch Vehicle (PSLV), in addition to a camera provided by the French space agency CNES.

2.4 International Roadmaps and Coordination

Beyond the dialogue taking place between partners in the frame of bilateral and multilateral programmes (e.g. ISS), the various international fora exist for exchanging information on national space exploration policies and plans, and for coordinating related activities.

- **International Space Exploration Coordination Group (ISECG)**: this is the space agencies' forum for advancing a common vision on the next steps for global space exploration. It has produced a Global Exploration Roadmap (GER) as a result of the joint work of 15 space agencies.
- **International Space Exploration Forum (ISEF)**: contrary to the ISECG which involves primarily space agencies, the ISEF is a ministerial-level international forum which maintains political dialogue on space exploration at the international government level.
- **United Nations Office for Outer Space Affairs (UNOOSA)**: As part of the United Nations framework, UNOOSA promotes international cooperation in the peaceful use and exploration of space, and in the utilization of space science and technology for sustainable economic and social development.

2.4.1 The International Space Exploration Coordination Group (ISECG)

The International Space Exploration Coordination Group (ISECG) was established in response to "The Global Exploration Strategy: The Framework for Coordination" developed by fourteen space agencies and released in May 2007. This long-term plan was derived from the attempt to create a consistent set of shared goals, concerning robotic and Human Exploration activities of the inner solar system.

The purpose of the ISECG is to work collectively towards further development and coordinate the global exploration strategy by:

- Providing a forum for participants to discuss their interests, objectives, and plans in space exploration, and
- Promoting interest and engagement in space exploration activities throughout society worldwide.

In August 2013, ISECG released the Global Exploration Roadmap (GER), turning the shared goals and objectives into a common roadmap. The common Mission Scenario identified a set of missions in the lunar vicinity and on the lunar surface that advance readiness for human Mars missions after 2030. Extended duration crew missions in the lunar vicinity and accessible asteroids will allow demonstration of the transportation, habitation, robotic servicing and other key systems on which long-duration missions into deep space must rely [40].

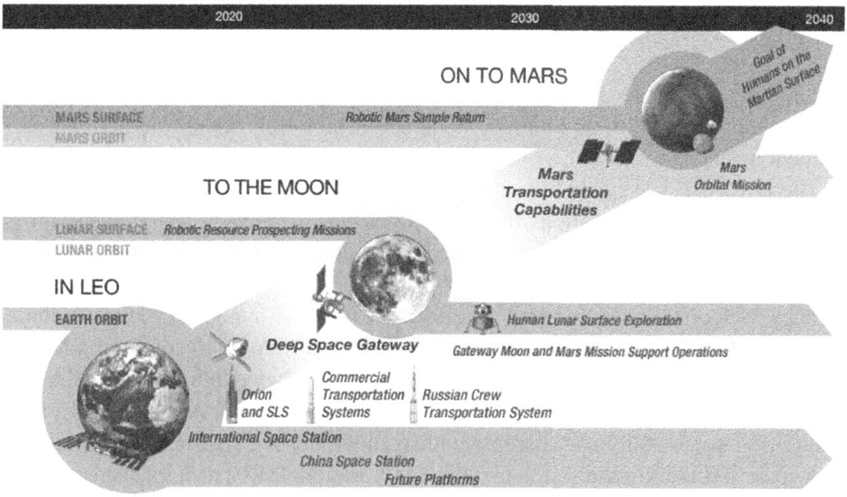

Fig. 2.6 Global exploration roadmap *Source* ISECG [41]

It is clear that within the ISECG community, space agencies aim to coordinate their investments in space exploration programmes and work together in ways that maximize the return on investments in institutional and commercial space activities. The expected benefits of establishing the ISECG are to increase cost-effectiveness of individual and collective exploration goals and to facilitate the ability of participating agencies to engage in productive bilateral or multilateral discussions.

In 2018, it was published the new Global Exploration Roadmap that reaffirmed the intention of 14 space agencies to expand "human presence into the solar system, with the surface of Mars as a common driving goal" [41]. It reflects the key objective to coordinate international effort to prepare space exploration missions beginning with ISS and continuing to the lunar vicinity and surface, then on to Mars (Fig. 2.6).

ISECG space agencies foresee that by the mid-2020s, a Gateway in the lunar vicinity will open the space frontier for Human Exploration of the Moon, Mars and asteroids. The support of governments, the private sectors and academia is considered fundamental to determine investments and partnerships that can "translate this blueprint into tangible progress extending human presence, with the associated benefits" [41].

What is important to underline is that the growing private sector interest in space exploration is already transforming the future of Low Earth Orbit, creating new opportunities as space agencies look to expand human presence into the solar system. Growing capability and interest from the private sector points out a future for collaboration not only among international space agencies but also with private entities pursuing their own goals and objectives, enabling new approaches and creating markets for services to support space exploration.

2.4.2 *The International Space Exploration Forum (ISEF)*

The International Space Exploration (ISEF) is a ministerial-level international forum and maintains the political dialogue on space exploration at the international government level.

The last ISEF was hosted by the USA in 2014. ISEF participants supported the work of space agencies participating in the ISECG in developing a strategic roadmap for human space exploration documented in the 2013 Global Exploration Roadmap released in August.

They welcomed an expansion of efforts to increase synergies between human and robotic missions to maximize their collective contribution to common goals and strategic partnerships. What is also noteworthy is that they explicitly recognized the growth in commercial spaceflight activities, making clear that private sector efforts could bring new vitality and disruptive ideas in the field of space exploration.

As part of this common vision for space exploration, ISEF participants recognized the growth in commercial spaceflight activities. They emphasized the importance of commercial spaceflight in exploration activities in accordance with existing national and international guidelines.

In addition, ISEF acknowledged that United Nations Committee on the Peaceful Uses of Outer Space (COPUOS) is "an important venue in which space-faring and non-space-faring nations alike can continue to discuss important issues regarding expanding humanity's horizons in space and furthering the objectives of the 1967 Treaty on Principles Governing the Activities of States in the Exploration and Use of Outer Space" [41].

2.4.3 *United Nations Committee on the Peaceful Use of Outer Space (COPUOS)*

The Committee on the Peaceful Uses of Outer Space (COPUOS) is an important international forum for international decision-making guidance, coordination and information dissemination. The Committee is considered a "natural platform for identifying a coordination mechanism to ensure that all States, both developed and developing, involving the private sector, civil society, and young generations, can participate in and benefit from space exploration and innovation:"[4]

At its fifty-ninth session in June 2016, the Committee endorsed the seven thematic priorities[5] of UNISPACE+50, their objectives, and mechanism. UNISPACE+50 aims to become a major milestone for designing a vision for the COPUOS and to strengthen

---

[4]Committee on the Peaceful Uses of Outer Space, UNISPACE+50 Thematic Priority 1: Global partnership in space exploration and innovation, Vienna, 7-16 June 2011.

[5]1. Global partnership in space exploration and innovation, 2. legal regime of outer space and global space governance, 3. enhanced information exchange on space objects and events, 4. international framework for space weather services, 5. strengthened space cooperation for global health, 6.

its unified the efforts at all levels and among all relevant stakeholders in shaping the global "Space 2030 agenda".[6]

In particular, the Thematic Priority 1, *Global partnership in space exploration and innovation,* aims to raise awareness of space exploration and innovation as important drivers for opening up new domains in: space science and technology, trigger new partnerships and promote cooperation which allows space exploration activities to become open and inclusive on the global scale.

At its fifty-ninth session, an *Action Team* has been established by the Committee as the mechanism to drive the Thematic Priority 1, coordinating space exploration. It works under the Co-Chairs of China, Jordan, and the USA, with the United Nations Office for Outer Space Affairs providing substantive and secretariat support [42].

The goal of the Action Team is to provide recommendations towards UNISPACE+50 that [42]:

- Raise awareness of and further advance space exploration and innovation, as essential drivers for opening up new domains in space science and technology,
- Advance proposals aimed at triggering new partnerships and models of partnership,
- Contribute to developing a dialogue between governmental and non-governmental entities engaged in space exploration,
- Promote cooperation, which allows space exploration activities to become open and inclusive on the global scale,
- Promote capacity building, in connection with space exploration and innovation, in particular for developing countries, and emerging space-faring nations, and
- Promote the engagement of youth in science, technology, engineering and mathematics within the context of space exploration and innovation, while recognizing that the benefits of such engagement extend far beyond the topic of space exploration and innovation.

References

1. European Space Agency, *Resolution on Europe's Space Exploration Strategy* (2014). Retrieved from ESA http://esamultimedia.esa.int/multimedia/publications/ESA_Space_Exploration_Strategy/offline/download.pdf
2. European Space Agency, *Exploring Together: ESA Space Exploration Strategy*. ESA/ESTEC (2015). Retrieved from ESA http://youbenefit.spaceflight.esa.int/esa-space-exploration-strategy/
3. Space Advisory Group of the European Commission, Framework Programme 7—Space Theme, *Space Exploration, a new European Flagship Programme* (2010). Retrieved from

international cooperation towards emission and resilent societies, 7. capacity building for the twenty-first century.

[6]The thematic priorities and their objectives were recommended by the Scientific and technical Subcommittee and at its fifty-third session and by the Legal Subcommittee at its fifty-fifth session, for further consideration by COPUOS at its fifty-ninth session. UNISPACE+50 thematic priorities and their long-term deliverables will align the 2030 Agenda for Sustainable Development.

https://ec.europa.eu/research/fp7/pdf/advisory-groups/sag_paper_on_space_exploration_october_2010.pdf
4. European Space Policy, *Space Exploration: European Ministers in Prague Prepare a Roadmap Towards a Common Vision* (2009). Retrieved from http://www.esa.int/Our_Activities/Human_Spaceflight/Space_exploration_European_Ministers_in_Prague_prepare_a_roadmap_towards_a_common_vision
5. European Commission, Proposal for a Regulation Of The European Parliament And Of The Council Establishing the Space Programme of the Union and the European Union Agency for the Space Programme and repealing Regulations (EU) No 912/2010, (EU) No 1285/2013, (EU) No 377/2014 and Decision 541/2014/EU (2018)
6. V. Reillon, *European Space Policy, Historical Perspective, Specific Aspects and Key*. EPRS| European Parliamentary Research Service (2017). Retrieved from http://www.europarl.europa.eu/RegData/etudes/IDAN/2017/595917/EPRS_IDA%282017%29595917_EN.pdf
7. European Space Agency. *ESA Budget for 2018* (2018). Retrieved from ESA http://www.esa.int/About_Us/Welcome_to_ESA/Funding
8. European Space Agency, *Ministerial Council 2016* (2016). Retrieved from ESA http://www.esa.int/About_Us/Ministerial_Council_2016/Human_Spaceflight_and_Robotic_Exploration_Programmes
9. European Space Agency, *Council Meeting Held at ministerial Level on 1 and 2 December 2016 Resolutions and Main Decisions* (2016). ESA. Retrieved from ESA https://esamultimedia.esa.int/docs/corporate/For_Public_Release_CM-16_Resolutions_and_Decisions.pdf
10. ESA, *Robotic Exploration* (2016). Retrieved from ESA http://exploration.esa.int/mars/48088-mission-overview/
11. European Space Agency. *ESA's plans for Lunar Exploration*. Retrieved from ESA https://www.hou.usra.edu/meetings/leag2014/presentations/carpenter.pdf
12. European Space Agency, *Council Meeting Held at Ministerial Level on 1 and 2 December 2016 Resolutions and Main Decisions* (2016). Lucerne. Retrieved from http://esamultimedia.esa.int/docs/corporate/For_Public_Release_CM-16_Resolutions_and_Decisions.pdf
13. Centre National d'Etudes Spatiales, *France–India Space Cooperation—Agreements Signed On Future Launchers and Lunar Exploration*. CNES (2017). Retrieved from https://presse.cnes.fr/en/france-india-space-cooperation-agreements-signed-future-launchers-and-lunar-exploration
14. Centre National d'Etudes Spatiales, *CNES and NASA Sign Cooperation Agreement On Mars 2020 Mission* (2016). Retrieved from CNES https://presse.cnes.fr/en/cnes-and-nasa-sign-cooperation-agreement-mars-2020-mission
15. C. Al-Ekabi, B. Baranes, P. Hulsroj, A. Lahecen, *Yearbook on Space Policy 2012/2013, Space in a Changing Word* (Springer, European Space Institute (ESPI), Vienna, 2013)
16. M. Wall, *President Obama's Space Legacy: Mars, Private Spaceflight and More* (2017). Space.Com. Retrieved from Space.com https://www.space.com/35394-president-obama-spaceflight-exploration-legacy.html
17. T. Malik, *Obama Budget Scraps NASA Moon Plan for '21st Century Space Program* (2010)'. Retrieved from Space.com https://www.space.com/7849-obama-budget-scraps-nasa-moon-plan-21st-century-space-program.html
18. K. Chang, *Space Council Chooses the Moon as Trump Administration Priority* (2017). Retrieved form The New York Times https://www.nytimes.com/2017/10/05/science/national-space-council-moon-pence.html
19. J. Foust, *National Space Council calls for human return to the moon* (2017). Retrieved from SpaceNEws http://spacenews.com/national-space-council-calls-for-human-return-to-the-moon/
20. NASA, *New Space Policy Directive Calls for Human Expansion Across Solar System* (2017). Retrieved from NASA https://www.nasa.gov/press-release/new-space-policy-directive-calls-for-human-expansion-across-solar-system
21. NASA, *NASA Strategic Plan 2018* (2018). Retrieved from https://www.nasa.gov/sites/default/files/atoms/files/nasa_2018_strategic_plan.pdf

22. U.S. Office of Management and Budget, *Budget of the U.S. Government—Fiscal Year 2019* (2018). Retrieved from https://www.whitehouse.gov/wp-content/uploads/2018/02/budget-fy2019.pdf
23. Space Foundation, *The Space Report 2017—The Authoritative Guide to Global Space Activity* (Space Foundation Offices, Colorado, 2017)
24. G. Williams, *Human Exploration Plans* (2017). Retrieved from NASA https://www.nasa.gov/sites/default/files/atoms/files/nac_exploration_july_2017_4-2.pdf
25. NASA, *NASA's Plans for Human Exploration Beyond Low Earth Orbit* (2017). Office of Inspector General. Retrieved from NASA https://oig.nasa.gov/audits/reports/FY17/IG-17-017.pdf
26. NASA, *Heomd-001 Initial Release Date: 09/07/2016 Human Exploration and Operations Exploration Objectives* (2016). Retrieved from https://www.nasa.gov/sites/default/files/atoms/files/heomd_001_-_exploration_objectives_baseline_release_090716.pdf
27. S. Scimemi, *International Space Station and ISS Transition* (2017). Retrieved from: https://www.nasa.gov/sites/default/files/atoms/files/nov_2017_nac_iss_status_and_transition_final.pdf
28. J. Foust, *Pondering the Future of the International Space Station* (2017). Retrieved from The Space Review http://www.thespacereview.com/article/3297/1
29. W.H. Gerstenmaier, *Progress in Defining the Deep Space Gateway and Transport Plan* (2017). Retrieved from NASA: https://www.nasa.gov/sites/default/files/atoms/files/heo_update.pdf
30. NASA, *Deep Space Gateway to Open Opportunities for Distant Destinations* (2017). Retrieved from NASA https://www.nasa.gov/feature/deep-space-gateway-to-open-opportunities-for-distant-destinations
31. NASA, *What's Next for NASA?* (2018). Retrieved from NASA https://www.nasa.gov/about/whats_next.html
32. M. Aliberti, *When China Goes to the Moon...ESPI* (Springer, Vienna, 2015)
33. C. Al-Ekabi, B. Banares, P. Hulsroj, A. Lahcen, *Yearbook on Space Policy 2012/2013: Space in a Changing World* (Springer, Vienna, 2013)
34. L. Grush, *Russia Announces Plans to Send Humans to the Moon in 2029* (2015). Retrieved from https://www.theverge.com/2015/10/28/9628952/roscosmos-crewed-lunar-mission-colony-2029-esa
35. T.A. Alwahed, *Roscosmos, NASA to Build 'Deep Space Gateway' Near Moon* (2017). Retrieved from The Guardian https://www.theguardian.com/science/2017/sep/27/russia-and-us-will-cooperate-to-build-moon-first-space-station
36. L. David, *China's Space Station Will Be Open to Science from All UN Nations* (2018). Retrieved from Space.Com https://www.space.com/40727-china-space-station-united-nations-experiments.html
37. F. Jeff, *Japan has Plans to Land Astronauts on the Moon by 2030—with a Little Help from the United States* (2017). Retrieved from Space News http://spacenews.com/mda-establishes-company-to-commercialize-satellite-servicing-technology/
38. JAXA, *NASA-JAXA Joint Statement on Space Exploration* (2018). Retrieved from JAXA http://global.jaxa.jp/press/2018/01/20180126_nasa.html
39. D. Goh, *JAXA and ESA to Study Feasibility of Lunar Demonstration Mission 'Heracles'* (2018). Retrieved from SpaceTech http://www.spacetechasia.com/jaxa-esa-study-feasibility-lunar-demonstration-mission-heracles/
40. ISECG, *The Global Exploration Roadmap* (2013). Retrieved from https://www.nasa.gov/sites/default/files/files/GER-2013_Small.pdf
41. ISECG, *The Global Exploration Roadmap* (2018). Retrieved from https://www.globalspaceexploration.org/wordpress/wp-content/isecg/GER_2018_small_mobile.pdf
42. Space Forum, *Action Team on Exploration and Innovation* (2017). Retrieved from http://space.aiaa.org/UN/

Chapter 3
The Evolving Role of Private Actors in Space Exploration

3.1 New Space: A Change of Paradigm

Space activities, and in particular space exploration and human spaceflight, have traditionally been driven by governments procuring space systems from a private industrial base usually through cost-plus contracts involving close scrutiny of operations by space agencies. Although the vast majority of space activities are still driven by governments with private industries acting as contractors for public programmes and relying massively on public funding, this *status quo* is being increasingly challenged with new opportunities for a more prominent contribution of commercial actors lying in the so-called New Space ecosystem.

In a recent study, ESPI investigated the New Space evolution and examined the various interrelated trends comprising this emerging business-driven shift [1]. As a result, ESPI defined New Space as "a disruptive sectorial dynamic featuring various end-to-end efficiency-driven concepts driving the space sector towards a more business- and service-oriented step". ESPI also isolated six trends which, together, characterize the New Space phenomenon (Fig. 3.1).

ESPI research underlined that endeavours and practices in the space sector have tangibly evolved over the last decade and continue to do so at a remarkably fast pace. This evolution is characterized by:

- **Innovative public procurement and support schemes** impacting deeply the relationship between public and private partners in the space sector. As a matter of fact, public strategies to foster commercial space activities have been instrumental in the emergence of the New Space ecosystem. It is actually the combination of both effective public strategies and favourable business conditions that fostered the trends observed today. These policies included in particular the implementation of new public procurement schemes building on a more prominent role and investment from private actors contrasting with traditional cost-plus contracts. These approaches enabled, in addition to cost and risk sharing, a radical optimization of

C. Iacomino, *Commercial Space Exploration*,
SpringerBriefs from the European Space Policy Institute,
https://doi.org/10.1007/978-3-030-15751-7_3

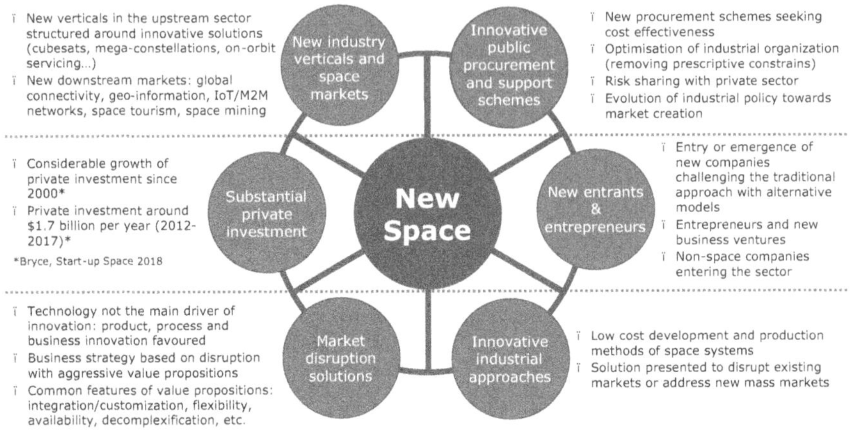

Fig. 3.1 Key trends driving the New Space sectorial dynamic

industrial organization by removing prescriptive constraints. In this new context, most agencies started or continue to adapt their strategy and industrial policy to foster the emergence of private endeavours, build partnerships and readjust their roles and procurement models. This is addressed in more detail in the next chapters.

- **New entrants** in the space sector falling in two categories: Non-space companies including in particular large ICT companies eager to expand their activities and build on cross-fertilization between ICT and space applications; New Space companies leveraging private and/or public funding to initiate innovative business models and address New Space markets or existing space markets with disruptive solutions. These new entrants challenge the traditional approach adopted in the sector for space programmes with new processes, business models or solutions.
- **Innovative industrial approaches** based on new processes, methods and industrial organization for the development and production of space systems or launchers. These innovative approaches aim principally at cutting down costs or explore new concepts with the underlying objective of creating the conditions either to disrupt existing markets or to address new ones. New techniques adopted by New Space players include, for example, industrial organization optimization, supply chain rationalization and vertical integration, miniaturization, proven technologies re-use, economies of scale, production line automation and digitization, standardized architectures or use of COTS among others.
- **Disruptive market solutions** offering, for example, new applications, integrated services, lower prices, reduced lead times, lower complexity or higher performance among other value proposition features; a large number of New Space endeavours proactively target the development of solutions with the capacity to disrupt existing space markets or address new ones. These solutions are not necessarily based on new technologies but rather on revisited concepts giving way to an alternative innovation dynamic. In general, New Space endeavours address well-

known shortcomings of the current space sector offer with promising solutions, but the profitability and sustainability of the related business models still have to be demonstrated.

- **Substantial private investment** from different sources and involving different funding mechanisms. The value of private investment in space businesses has noticeably increased, in line with the growing number of new companies and start-ups. This is more particularly true in the USA. Various sources of investment exist including private fortunes, venture capital firms, business angels, private equity companies or banks. On average, $1.7 billion was invested annually in space start-ups during the period 2012–2017. Focused on the development of business ventures, private investment complements well public budgets by addressing short-term industrial objectives and supporting start-up and scale-up phases. This creates new opportunities to foster the emergence and growth of commercial endeavours and to support industry competitiveness and innovation.
- **New industry verticals and space markets** targeting the provision of New Space applications. An important share of new entrants is developing business models around new industry verticals and space markets. In the downstream part of the value chain, various promising new markets have been identified for business venture including, for example, global connectivity, geo-information services, space tourism or, in the longer-term, space mining. The provision of such new services requires specific systems which, in turn, impact upstream activities with the development of specific solutions. Among the growing upstream verticals, the skyrocketing number of small spacecraft, including, for example, CubeSats or mega-Constellations, has created a momentum for businesses interested in providing dedicated solutions (e.g. microlaunchers, miniaturized systems, COTS). Here also the economic viability of these new markets remains uncertain today.

Together, these interrelated trends are driving a profound paradigm shift in the space sector leading to new opportunities for commercial space ventures and private contributions to public space programmes in various space fields including, in particular, space exploration and human spaceflight. As a matter of fact, these two domains have been substantially impacted by the New Space evolution with outstanding achievements of public strategies and the emergence of various private endeavours pursuing the goal to conduct business in these fields.

Fostering the involvement of commercial actors in public programmes is nowadays a dominant consideration of governments and agencies who are increasingly eager to explore new mechanisms to take advantage of private contributions to engage in future programmes and achieve challenging space exploration goals. In general, various announcements and institution-led initiatives such as ESA Calls for Ideas to trigger a commercial utilization of the ISS, underline the increasing interest of space agencies in opening exploration programmes to commercial contributions and reap associated benefits. Closely related to New Space ecosystem, this new context creates programmatic opportunities and challenges for space agencies.

The following chapters examine the public and private sides of this evolving landscape looking into:

- **Public strategies**, in Europe and the USA, to foster the development of commercial space activities and to integrate a more prominent contribution of the private sector to public programmes through new mechanisms;
- **Private sector trends** in space exploration including, in particular, the emergence of new ventures based on innovative business models and the growth of private investment in the sector.

3.2 Public Strategies to Foster and Leverage Private Contributions

3.2.1 Approach to Commercial Space Exploration in the USA

3.2.1.1 US Strategy to Foster Commercial Space

The American effort to foster commercial space activities and markets is a long-standing one that started as soon as 1962 with the Communications Satellite Act which enabled private companies to own and operate satellites. This effort gained a new dimension under Reagan administration with the Commercial Space Launch Act of 1984 which "recognized the US private sector as having the capability to develop commercial launch vehicles, orbital satellites, and operate private launch sites and services" [2].

With the objective to encourage a more prominent investment and involvement of private actors in space activities in line with Reagan vision of "new frontier" of economic development, multiple legal initiatives in various domains further defined and expanded the perimeter of commercial space. This continuous effort was first and foremost motivated by the opportunity to conciliate American leadership and reduction of government budgets. Over the years, fostering a commercial space activity has become an integral component of US space strategy supported at the highest political level. Reagan administration's plan to use the Space Shuttle as a commercial launcher was the first step that indirectly linked US human spaceflight and space exploration programmes and in particular the ISS, to the US commercial space strategy.

In the field of space exploration, US long-standing and continuous effort to support the emergence of a private space industry further intensified at the beginning of the twenty-first century with a series of acts adopted under Bush, Obama and Trump administrations. In 2004, President George W. Bush announced a *Vision for Space Exploration* directing NASA to "pursue commercial opportunities for providing transportation and other services supporting the International Space Station and exploration missions beyond Low Earth Orbit" [3]. The US Congress endorsed this vision and adopted the NASA Authorization Act of 2005 which explicitly directed NASA Administrator to "develop a commercialization plan to support the human missions to the Moon and Mars and to support Low Earth Orbit activities" [2] and in particular to "acquire cargo transportation as soon as practical and affordable to support missions to and from the International Space Station". It is in this context and in view of replacing the ageing and costly Space Shuttle that Bush administration laid the foundations of the Commercial Orbital Transportation Services (COTS) programme which relied on the commercial space sector for the servicing of the ISS.

Obama administration marked a turn from the Bush administration for various important elements of the US space exploration programme but further consolidated US engagement with private companies in the field. Under the Obama administration, the role of private actors to lower space programme costs, restore NASA human spaceflight capabilities and reaffirm US independence in space became central [4]. NASA Authorization Act of 2010 explicitly approved NASA plans to work with private companies to develop commercial spaceflight capabilities to deliver both cargo and crew to the ISS [5]. Another key initiative under the Obama administration is the adoption of the Spurring Private Aerospace Competitiveness and Entrepreneurship (SPACE) Act (i.e. or US Commercial Space Launch Competitiveness Act) of 2015. This Act updated US commercial space legislation in the field of private spaceflight and space resources exploitation, expanding the realm of commercial space activities.

Trump administration marked again a turn from Obama plans and restored Bush Constellation programme vision, but the willingness to further involve commercial actors in public programmes remained a dominant consideration. The NASA Transition Authorization Act of 2017 places much emphasis on the importance of the commercial space industry in various domains including in particular human spaceflight and space exploration. The bill acknowledges the achievements of the COTS programme and supports its continuity but also emphasizes the importance of using the ISS as a platform to foster commercialization and economic development of Low Earth Orbit. At various occasions, the Act directs NASA to continue its effort to engage in ambitious partnerships with the private industry.

During its first meeting in October 2017, the National Space Council marked another important step in solidifying US continuous commitment to foster commercial space activities. Mark Albrecht, who was executive secretary of the Council from 1989 to 1992, underlined that "the agenda [of the National Space Council] will be substantial and urgent, from rationalizing space launch to fully integrating new privatized and commercial space capabilities into all national space activities" [6].

Currently, the Trump administration aims to turn the station "into a kind of orbiting real estate venture run not by the government, but by private industry" [7]. What is important to underline is the clear intention to work on a transition plan that could turn the ISS over to the private sector, according to an internal NASA document obtained by The Washington Post. Despite the cessation of the direct US Federal funding for ISS in 2025, this decision does not imply that the platform itself will be deorbited at that time, but the intention is to secure the nation's long-term presence in LEO orbit, partnering with industry to develop commercial orbital platforms and capabilities that the private sector and NASA can use [8].

In its budget request, the administration requested \$150 million in the fiscal year 2019, with more in the next years "to encourage the development of new commercial

Low Earth Orbital platforms and capabilities for use by the private sector and NASA" [9] (Table 3.1).

The current administration has the clear purpose to push that public–private partnership even further to encourage "the emergence of an environment in LEO orbit where NASA is one of many customers of a non-governmental human spaceflight managed and operated enterprise, while providing a smooth and uninterrupted transition" [11].

The first strategic goal of *NASA Strategic Plan 2018* is based on the purpose to improve scientific research in order to open the pathway for exploration and robotic–human partnerships. For this purpose, the ISS, considered as "an orbital outpost for humanity, has the key functionality for global cooperation and scientific advancement, as a catalyst for growing new commercial marketplaces in space and as a test bed for demonstrating advanced technologies". In this context, NASA plans to extend partnerships domestically and internationally.

The second goal concerns the aim "to pursue a sustainable cadence of missions with the aim to prepare the first crewed missions to deep space" [11]. These include the first test flight of the SLS and Orion crew vehicle near the Moon and the first crewed flight of this transportation system, designed for missions beyond LEO orbit. However, beyond the recent commercial crew and cargo transportation capabilities enabled by the ISS, the agency is continually implementing and developing a new partnership approach to further allow commercial activities and markets in LEO orbit [12]. To support LEO orbit commercialization, NASA is leveraging the ISS by maximizing utilization and demonstrating the value of ISS and LEO research. For this strategy, the agency is enabling commercial use of ISS by offering its capabilities and providing Earth-similar laboratory capabilities. Additionally, NASA is addressing the policy environment and associated elimination of barriers and introduction of incentives that could enable commercial use of LEO orbit. To realize NASA's vision of a self-sustaining market in LEO orbit, the agency has created the Commercial Development Programme to directly expand commercial activities with a focus on enabling and developing commercial platforms that can be used by NASA and other customers [13].

The third goal concerns the challenges that the agency is addressing such as gathering climate change data; supplying technological solutions for terrestrial problems; advancing the state of research and development (R&D) in aeronautics and other fields; developing commercial and human space launch and transportation capabilities; understanding cosmic phenomena as wide-ranging as space weather, asteroids and exoplanets; and improving the nation's innovation capacity. In particular, through investments within the Exploration Research & Technology (ER&T) funding account, the Agency will advance important technologies for both NASA mission challenges and national needs and also address the market challenges related to providing state-of-the-art commercial space. More specifically, technology investments within the ER&T funding account will focus on [8]:

- Accelerating large-scale industrialization of space,
- Enabling efficient and safe transportation into and through space,

Table 3.1 FY 2019 budget request ($M)

Budget authority ($ in millions)	Fiscal year						
				Notional			
	2017	2018	2019	2020	2021	2022	2023
NASA Total	$19,653.3	$19,519.8	$19,892.2	$19,592.2	$19,592.2	$19,592.2	$19,592.2
Deep space exploration systems	$4,164.0	$4,222.6	$4,558.8	$4,859.1	$4,764.5	$4,752.5	$4,769.8
Exploration systems development	$3,929.0		$3,669.8	$3,790.5	$3,820.2	$3,707.5	$3,845.6
Advanced exploration systems	$97.8		$889.0	$1,068.6	$944.3	$1,045.0	$924.1
Exploration research and development	$157.2		$0.0	$0.0	$0.0	$0.0	$0.0
Exploration research and technology	$826.5	$820.8	$1,002.7	$912.7	$912.7	$912.7	$912.7
LEO and spaceflight operations	$4,942.5	$4,850.1	$4,624.6	$4,273.7	$4,393.3	$4,430.3	$4,438.0
International Space Station	$1,450.9		$1,462.2	$1,453.2	$1,471.2	$1,466.2	$1,451.2
Space transportation	$2,589.0		$2,108.7	$1,829.1	$1,858.9	$1,829.2	$1,807.3
Space and flight support (SES)	$902.6		$903.7	$841.4	$888.2	$934.9	$954.6
Commercial LEO development	$0.0		$150.0	$150.0	$175.0	$200.0	$225.0
Science	$5,762.2	$5,725.8	$5,895.0	$5,859.9	$5,841.1	$5,822.4	$5,803.6
Earth science	$1,907.7		$1,784.2	$1,784.2	$1,784.2	$1,784.2	$1,784.2
Planetary science	$1,827.5		$2,234.7	$2,199.6	$2,180.8	$2,162.1	$2,143.3
Astrophysics	$1,352.3		$1,185.4	$1,185.4	$1,185.4	$1,185.4	$1,185.4
Heliophysics	$674.7		$690.7	$690.7	$690.7	$690.7	$690.7

(continued)

Table 3.1 (continued)

Budget authority ($ in millions)	Fiscal year						
				Notional			
	2017	2018	2019	2020	2021	2022	2023
Aeronautics	$656.0	$655.5	$633.9	$608.9	$608.9	$608.9	$608.9
Education	$100.0	$99.3	$0.0	$0.0	$0.0	$0.0	$0.0
Safety, security and mission services	$2,768.6	$2,749.8	$2,749.7	$2,744.8	$2,738.6	$2,732.3	$2,726.1
Centre management and operations	$1,986.5		$1,949.6	$1,945.4	$1,939.8	$1,934.1	$1,928.5
Agency management and operations	$782.1		$800.1	$799.4	$798.8	$798.2	$797.6
Construction and environmental compliance restoration	$375.6	$358.3	$388.2	$293.8	$293.8	$293.8	$293.8
Construction of facilities	$305.4		$305.3	$210.9	$210.9	$210.9	$210.9
Environmental compliance and restoration	$70.2		$82.9	$82.9	$82.9	$82.9	$82.9
Inspector general	$37.9	$37.6	$39.3	$39.3	$39.3	$39.3	$39.3
NASA total	$19,653.3	$19,519.8	$19.892.2	$19,592.2	$19,592.2	$19,592.2	$19,592.2

Source NASA [10]

- Increasing access to planetary surfaces,
- Enabling humans to live and work in space and on planetary surfaces,
- Expanding capabilities through robotic exploration and discovery,
- Growing and utilizing the US industrial and academic base products and services.

The ER&T investment portfolios span a range of discipline areas and Technology Readiness Levels to advance technologies for the benefit of NASA, industry and other public agencies. Through the ER&T account, NASA invests in transformational exploration technologies with the potential to balance risk, moderate cost and advance critical capabilities for future exploration missions and broader national needs [14].

Finally, with the fourth goal, NASA has a particular focus on optimizing its technical capabilities. As a result, NASA has assumed "a new operating model that strengthens its management of the engineering and systems capabilities that are fundamental to every mission and strategic goal" [8]. NASA aims to leverage innovation outside the agency. For this purpose, NASA is developing a robust partnership and acquisition strategy focused on cooperating with the private sectors in order to benefit from their innovations. These principles embrace a "shared understanding of the responsible use of space, free and open data policies, and the broad benefits of fundamental public research and development (R&D)" [8].

What is important in this context is the clear objective for NASA to engage in more ambitious partnership strategies. These partnerships will implement mutually beneficial cooperative space working groups, programmes, projects, missions and ground-based research activities that support the Strategic Plan [8].

3.2.1.2 Public Instruments to Foster and Leverage Private Contributions in the USA

In line with this strategy, multiple initiatives were launched by the US government to foster the emergence and growth of a commercial space sector such as the establishment of an Office of Commercial Space Transportation (OCST) within the US Department of Transportation in 1984 to process private sector requests to obtain licences to operate expendable launch vehicle. In addition, the Commercial Amendment Act of 2004 providing guidelines for regulating the safety of commercial human spaceflight and the last Commercial Space Launch Competitiveness Act (2015) facilitating commercial exploitation of space resources by American citizens were considered important steps to develop the commercial sector.

The pro-commercialization US space strategy also fostered the emergence of various NASA initiatives laying the foundation of increasingly more ambitious relationships and partnerships with industry and the commercial sector. Already in 1984, NASA established an Office of Commercial Programmes that "encouraged the private sector to become more involved in using space for commercial purposes and increased NASA's efforts to find private sector uses for NASA-developed technology" [15].

An essential step having profoundly impacted the relationship between public and private actors came as a result of the Space Shuttle retirement. The reusable vehicle was initially "envisioned as a reliable, low-cost method of launching governmental and commercial payloads into orbit"[1] but these objectives were not entirely achieved for a variety of reasons (e.g. restrictions following the Challenger disaster in 1986 led to a launch rate significantly lower than expected, refurbishment operations much more expensive than initially anticipated …). Between 1971 and 2011, NASA spent around $192 billion in the programme for an average cost per launch between $1.2 and $1.5 billion [16]. The programme was terminated during the Bush administration in 2011 leaving the USA in a critical and costly situation of dependence on Russian capabilities and requiring a quick and cost-effective replacement.

NASA explains that, since its foundation in 1958, the agency "focused on government-owned and -operated space missions. Throughout the Mercury, Gemini, Apollo, and Space Shuttle programmes, the space agency hired contractors to develop launch vehicles and spacecraft."[2] As a result, private actors had been involved in NASA programmes almost exclusively as contractors through cost-plus contracts "based upon the actual cost of production and any agreed upon rates of profit or fees" [17]. This approach is traditionally applied for public procurement, even outside the space sector, to enable a close control over contractors operations and to ensure that public money is not spent to create outstanding profits. Although this approach lays on robust arguments, it is often pointed out as a source of cost overruns related to administrative burdens and an indirect incentive for selected contractors to maximize the cost of the programme as they get a percentage [18]. The replacement of the Space Shuttle provided a fertile ground for NASA to explore new mechanisms building on various prior initiatives resulting from NASA and industry effort to proactively seek alternatives to traditional NASA-industry relations, including in particular public–private partnerships and new contracting schemes.

The Commercial Orbital Transportation Services (COTS) model, developed and successfully executed by the Commercial Crew and Cargo Program (C3PO), has proven an example of a new way for how NASA can cooperate with private industry. With the overarching objective to improve cost-effectiveness and share development and operations risks with private actors, NASA implemented an innovative procurement scheme based on competitive, performance-based and fixed-price milestone. With fixed-price milestones, payments would only be guaranteed after the completion of predefined objectives, not on a continual basis as is customary under the system of a cost-plus contract in which companies are awarded a contract for the total cost of the work performed, plus an additional amount for profit. In other words, funding was issued only after the completion of predefined objectives, and any cost overruns would be the financial responsibility of the company, not the government [19].

---

[1] The amortization is paying off an amount owed over time by making planned, incremental payments of principal and interest.

[2] Commercial Orbital Transportation Services: A New Era in Spaceflight—Lyndon B. Johnson Space Centre Staff.

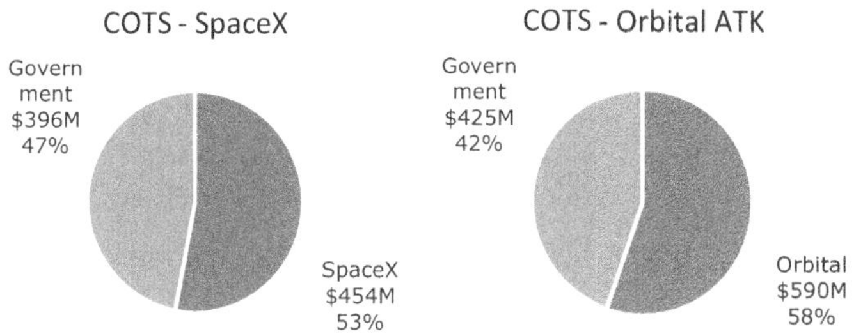

Fig. 3.2 Government-funding sources covered less than 50% of the development costs of SpaceX and Orbital transportation systems. *Source* NASA [19]

These programmes introduced a new way of doing business in the human spaceflight domain that made a mark in US national space history, creating a symbiotic relationship between the public and private sectors. To provide financial and technical resources to commercial companies, the COTS programme heavily relied on funded Space Act Agreements (SAA), a type of legal agreement that had already been envisaged in the National Aeronautics and Space Act of 1958 (and subsequent congressional authorizations) [20] and on the basis of which NASA can enter into partnerships with private companies, other government agencies and universities, giving access to a wider range of technologies and capabilities that are not part of NASA's core competency. For the COTS programme, terms and conditions of this mechanism were specially crafted to optimize mutual benefits for NASA and commercial partners. The primary aim of these agreements was to improve and stimulate the commercial space industry to develop innovative and cost-effective space transportation capabilities.

The advantage of the COTS SAAs was to "enable a portfolio investment in multiple and diverse commercial partners" with "the ability to fund a range of companies including large, established companies representing lower technical risk balances by small or emerging companies with higher risk" [20].

An important feature of these innovative partnership models sought by the government was the achievement of a high return on investment from taxpayer funds. For example, SpaceX and Orbital Low Earth Orbit transportation systems were developed with a total NASA COTS investment of just $788 million. NASA had provided less than "one half of the cost for the commercial transportation systems development and demonstration" [20] (as seen in Fig. 3.2).

COTS SAAs have been considered "as a new way of fostering interaction between NASA and the private sector" [21], different from traditional Federal Acquisition Regulations (FAR) cost-plus contracts, and eventually proved to be a successful tool to engage into partnership with private actors.

The application of the SAAs in COTS and Commercial Crew Development (CCDev) has meant the shifting of design and development to the contracted firm. Key milestones and the associated priced are defined by the private contractor and this aspect means that they "must deliver on time or not get paid" [21]. In this way,

Table 3.2 Change of paradigm at NASA

Programme characteristic	Early space age approach	Commercial-oriented approach
Owner	NASA	Industry
Contract fee-type	Cost-plus	Fixed price
Contract management	Prime contractor	Public–private partnership
Customer(s)	NASA	Government and non-government
Funding for capability demonstration	NASA procures capability	NASA provides investment via milestone payments
NASA's role in capability development	NASA defines "what" and "how"	NASA defines "what" industry defines "how"
Requirements' definition	NASA defines detailed requirements	NASA defines top-level capabilities needed
Cost structure	NASA incurs total cost	NASA and industry share cost

Source NASA [22]

the company has more freedom to define and deliver a service or technical capability and the NASA's involvement in the process is reduced as a broader reduction in cost, shifting some of the risks away from the agency.

The success of this innovative procurement approach paved the way for a partial but profound transformation of NASA relationship with industry. According to Gary Martins, former director of partnerships at NASA Ames Research Center, this paradigm shift can be summarized along the following criteria (Table 3.2).

Building on the successful legacy of COTS, in early 2014 the Advanced Exploration Systems Division (AES) in NASA's Human Exploration and Operations Mission Directorate began several initiatives to continue partnerships with the commercial space industry. Currently, NASA's AES division is fostering innovative approaches and public–private partnerships to rapidly develop prototype systems, advance key capabilities and validate operational concepts for future human missions beyond Earth orbit [23]. By engaging in strategic partnerships with private space actors and space agencies, AES is able to advance new technologies, reduce risk and reduce the cost for partners involved.

In addition to developing building blocks for future missions, the AES division is pioneering innovative ways to drive rapid progress by engaging in mutually beneficial public–private partnerships and educational:

- **Cost-sharing model** that allows the government and private companies to pool investments in a shared venture.
- **Student Challenges** that develop partnerships and collaborations with universities, high schools and non-profit organizations to help bridge gaps and increase knowledge in architectural design trades, capabilities and technology risk reduction related to NASA's strategic goals.

- **Small Business Partnerships** programmes provide an opportunity for small high-technology companies and research institutions (RI) to participate in government-sponsored research and development (R&D) efforts in key technology areas [24].

Particular initiatives were developed under a cost-sharing model, such as Lunar Cargo Transportation and Landing by Soft Touchdown (CATALYST), Commercial Lunar Payload Services (CPLS), Next Space Technologies for Exploration Partnerships (NextSTEP) and prize and competitions.

The CATALYST programme's purpose is to encourage and facilitate the development of US commercial robotic lunar cargo delivery capabilities. NASA's CATALYST initiative has created partnerships with three US companies to support the development of lunar lander technologies and capabilities, and one of the economics research proposals selected plans to assess and analyse the potential for commercial lunar efforts. In particular, NASA awarded three no-funds-exchanged SAAs partnerships with Astrobotic Technology, Masten Space Systems and Moon Express [25]. Those companies are developing landers that will be ready for missions within the next years. Astrobotic is planning its first Peregrine lander mission in 2019, while Moon Express expects to launch its MX-1E lander in 2018. Finally, Masten Space Systems is working on its XL-1 lander that could be ready by the end of the decade as well. However, the purpose of these SAAs is to encourage the development of robotic lunar landers that can be integrated with US commercial launch capabilities to deliver payloads to the lunar surface. In this way, NASA has the possibility to share technical expertise, access to facilities, equipment loans and software to stimulate the development of commercial lunar cargo transportation service.

Following the CATALYST programme, NASA released in April 2018 a Request for Proposal in order to boost the commercial US space industry harbouring new technologies to deliver payloads to the Moon. The Commercial Lunar Payload Services (CPLS) would lighten the agency's efforts to accelerate a robotic return to the Moon as the initial phase of a long-term exploration path. The CPLS mission is the first PPP in the deep space exploration domain. In November of the same year, nine private companies were selected:

- Astrobotic Technology,
- Deep Space Systems,
- Draper,
- Firefly Aerospace,
- Intuitive Machines,
- Lockheed Martin Space,
- Masten Space Systems,
- Moon Express,
- Orbit Beyond.

Allowed to bid on contracts, the companies can contemplate a combined maximum contract value of $2.6 billion in 10 years. The landers would be capable of sample return, resource prospecting, demonstrating use of in-space resources, primarily to reduce the risk when building landers for humans. It is worth to note the fluctuating level of company maturity and expertise, from big player such as Lockheed Martin, to green start-ups. Undoubtedly, it is a clear sign of confidence in the US industry capability to meet the needs of the 2019 mission. NASA plans to select 8–12 experiments next year for launch and with an overall budget of between $24 and 36 million in the first year of the programme. The agency is looking for ideas contributing to the commercial development of the Moon and advance, at the meantime, science capabilities. Hoping to send two payloads each year for the next 10 years, NASA promised to re-examine the private market periodically for new lunar capabilities and, perhaps, offer an on-ramping contract. In February 2019, NASA made the announcement of the selection of 12 demonstration payloads eligible to fly through the CPLS programme, including a range of scientific instruments. Those mature-enough selected payloads were carefully chosen in parallel with an outside agency call, the Lunar Surface Instrument and Technology Payload (LSITP), an upcoming selection. Before the LSITP disclosure, at the Washington Space Business Roundtable, Astrobotic and Moon Express executives expressed their concerns about the time feasibility of their first missions, supposedly ready to launch in 2020/2021. While NASA is looking at ways for acceleration, the start-ups are leaving open doors to minimize risks, like opting for a precursor orbiter in Moon Express' case, and be on-track.

Concerning the NASA announcement for NextSTEP, the agency was looking for ways to stimulate the commercial development of technologies that might have future applications for NASA's exploration plans. This public–private partnership model seeks commercial development of deep space exploration capabilities with the objective to support more extensive human spaceflight missions in the Proving Ground around and beyond cis-lunar space. Along these years, NASA issued two NextSTEP Broad Agency Announcements (BAA)[3] to US industry: one in late 2014, and the second NextSTEP BAA in April 2016.

With regard to the first NextSTEP, the selection included Bigelow Aerospace, Boeing, Lockheed Martin, Orbital ATK and seven other companies. The purpose is to advance concept studies and technology development projects in the areas of advanced propulsion, habitation and small satellites. Under the second NextSTEP, NASA awarded contracts to six big and small companies: Bigelow Aerospace, Boeing, Lockheed Martin, Orbital ATK, Sierra Nevada Corporation (SNC) and NanoRacks. The agreements are structured as cost-sharing deals where each company covers at least 30% of the cost [26]. The goal of these partnerships was to study designs for Deep Space Habitats that NASA could use in cis-lunar space. NASA estimated the combined total of all the awards, covering work in 2016 and 2017, would be approximately $65 million, with additional efforts and funding continuing into 2018 [27].

As part of NextSTEP-2, NASA released a solicitation to seek proposals from industry for the conduct of studies in specific research areas. Among these areas, NASA solicited proposals for the Power and Propulsion Element of the Deep Space

[3]Broad Agency Announcements (BAAs) are a procurement tool used by USAID to collaborate with the private and public sectors when facing a development challenge that does not have a clear solution and there appears to be an opportunity for innovation.

Gateway (Appendix C Power and Propulsion Element Studies). The Power and Propulsion Element would be the first module of the gateway launched, flying on the Exploration Mission (EM-2) launch of the Space Launch System along with Orion spacecraft. That announcement sought proposals for short-term studies to address technical issues involving the PPE, including its power and propulsion systems as well as other key subsystems [28]. In November 2017, NASA awarded contracts to five companies (Boeing, Lockheed Martin, Orbital ATK, Sierra Nevada Space Systems and Space Systems Loral) to examine how they could develop a power and propulsion module that could become the initial element of the Deep Space Gateway. The contracts, which run for four months, have a combined value of approximately $2.4 million [29].

The use of prizes, competition and crowdsourcing has played an important role in stimulating innovation and helping NASA solve problems. These mechanisms offer competitive award and the use of crowdsourcing solicits products, services, ideas or content contributions from many people, oftentimes (but not necessarily) through the Internet. The prizes shift the risk to the competitors based on challenges set by the agency, subsidizing the winner and providing a means for gathering and testing ideas from outside of NASA.

The NASA Centennial Challenges programme engages the public in the process of advanced technology development and offers incentive prizes to generate revolutionary solutions to problems of interest to NASA and the nation, stimulating or creating new business ventures. The programme seeks innovations from diverse and non-traditional sources.

Another mechanism, in line with the request of the White House Office of Science and Technology, is the Center of Excellence for Collaborative Innovation (CoECI). All CoECI challenges are managed under the umbrella of the NASA Tournament Lab (NTL). In particular, the Pavilion programme, managed by Tournament Lab, provides the opportunity to develop innovative solutions to the challenges faced by NASA in achieving its mission to pioneer the future of space exploration, scientific discovery and aeronautics research.

3.2.2 Approach to Commercial Space Exploration in Europe

3.2.2.1 European Strategy to Foster Commercial Space

Europe has actually been a pioneer in developing commercial space activities and building on a prominent role of the private sector. Already in the late 70s, Europe launched several initiatives to foster the emergence of a private and commercial space sector with outstanding success. For example, Arianespace, founded in 1980, was the world's first private space launch operator and SPOT Image, founded in 1982, was the first commercial operator and dealer for space imagery. Since then, European agencies and institutions engaged in an increasing number of ambitious commercial incentives and public–private partnerships in different fields (ARTES programme, TerraSAR-X, RapidEye and HYLAS project). Not all attempts were successful and, for example, the private concession model envisaged initially by the European Union for its flagship Galileo programme was eventually abandoned for a variety of reasons. Nevertheless, similarly to the USA, promoting and building on deep and continuous collaboration between private and public sectors to share costs and risks, pool expertise, share knowledge and ultimately foster competitiveness and economic growth is a central component of the European space strategy.

In the Space Strategy for Europe of 2016, the European Commission highlights its key objective to foster a globally competitive and innovative European space sector to maintain and further strengthen a world-class capacity to conceive, develop, launch, operate and exploit space systems and open up new opportunities to develop innovative products, services and processes which can benefit industry in all Member States. To achieve this objective, the Union intends to explore two areas:

- **Supporting research and innovation and development of skills**: based on dialogues with private actors and other innovation actors to address their competitiveness needs strengthen the use of innovative procurement schemes. The aim is to stimulate and support the demand-side of innovation and explore new approaches to leverage private sector investments and partnerships with industry;
- **Fostering entrepreneurship and new business opportunities**: the objective is to support European space entrepreneurs in starting and scaling up across the European single market, enhancing its support to small- and medium-sized enterprises (SMEs), start-ups and young entrepreneurs through business incubators and the use of prizes and competitions.

With regard to ESA, the Resolution on the Evolution of the Agency, approved in 2014 at Ministerial level, gave strong emphasis on the evolution of ESA's relations with Industry. Member States urged ESA Director General to make proposals for the next ESA Council meeting in 2016, promoting opportunities and innovative ways to adapt the relationship between ESA and industry in cooperative endeavours. The follow-up Resolution "*Towards Space 4.0 for a United Space in Europe*", adopted in 2016, addressed this demand with a clear intention to open up the agency to new partnerships with private actors in both space and non-space sectors and to implement complementary new funding schemes relying on commercial activities [30].

In this Resolution, ESA provided detailed objectives for its long-term industrial policy plan [30]:

- Fostering competitiveness, innovation and balanced development of the European industrial sector among all Member States, while also facilitating the entry of new economic actors and the integration of its latest Member States
- Supporting private investment and entrepreneurship, in particular through start-ups and SMEs, and carrying out the SME-friendly policy adopted by the Industrial Policy Committee (IPC) so as to favour their contribution to the success of ESA programmes
- Promoting public–private partnership schemes that include the sharing of risks and rewards, prioritizing pre-operational space activities with a potential for industrialization and commercialization

These objectives have been well addressed in ESA Space Exploration Strategy and E3P. In line with the vision of a "United Space in Europe" in the Space 4.0 framework, ESA aims to pursue a consistent and forward-looking space exploration programme designed to "further stimulate commercial partnerships with industrial entities" [30]. From this perspective, David Parker, ESA Director of Human Spaceflight and Robotic Exploration, commented that "commercial partnership will play a growing role in the exciting ESA vision for space exploration and (…) ESA intends to stimulate private sector engagement in space exploration and foster innovative and inspiring approaches for ISS services and utilization and future ESA missions" [30]. In addition to its regular space agencies' activities, ESA is increasingly willing to act as a business partner. In the field of space exploration, the objective of commercial partnerships is to facilitate exploration ambitions by better leveraging European private sector capabilities and resources. Consistent with the ESA's Space Exploration Strategy, the partnerships' idea is related, but not limited, to four areas of interest [31]:

- User-driven exploitation of Low Earth Orbit infrastructures
- Lunar and Mars exploration
- Joint research and development
- Inspiration.

3.2.2.2 Public Instruments to Foster and Leverage Private Contributions in Europe

New ESA Instruments

The New Space economy, described before, set up an adequate ecosystem providing a favourable ground for the implementation of ambitious public–private partnerships. From this standpoint, European-led initiatives to support innovation and development of private ventures, such as ESA Business Incubator Centers, Calls for Ideas, Grand Challenges, SME instruments and the cooperation with investment banks and venture capitalists, are important steps towards a renewed European approach.

Joerg Kreisel, specialist in investment in space ventures, affirmed that: "thanks in particular to initiatives as ESA Technology Transfer Programme (TTP)[4] and Business Incubation Centres (BIC), not only Europe can today boast a large number of start-ups being launched every year, but also an increasingly large networks of brokers, business angels, incubators, mentors and accelerators as well as university, research centres and experts" [32].

Figure 3.3 shows the current ESA BICs network which includes 16 European locations and focuses on the facilitation of the use of space technologies, systems and know-how, especially for non-space applications. Whit this objective, new ESA BIC launched in Finland implemented a new model to better foster synergies between

[4]Note: ESA TTP objective to bring space technologies down to Earth. The programme offers access to existing space technologies, expertise, patents, data and services to entrepreneurs, start-ups and SMEs.

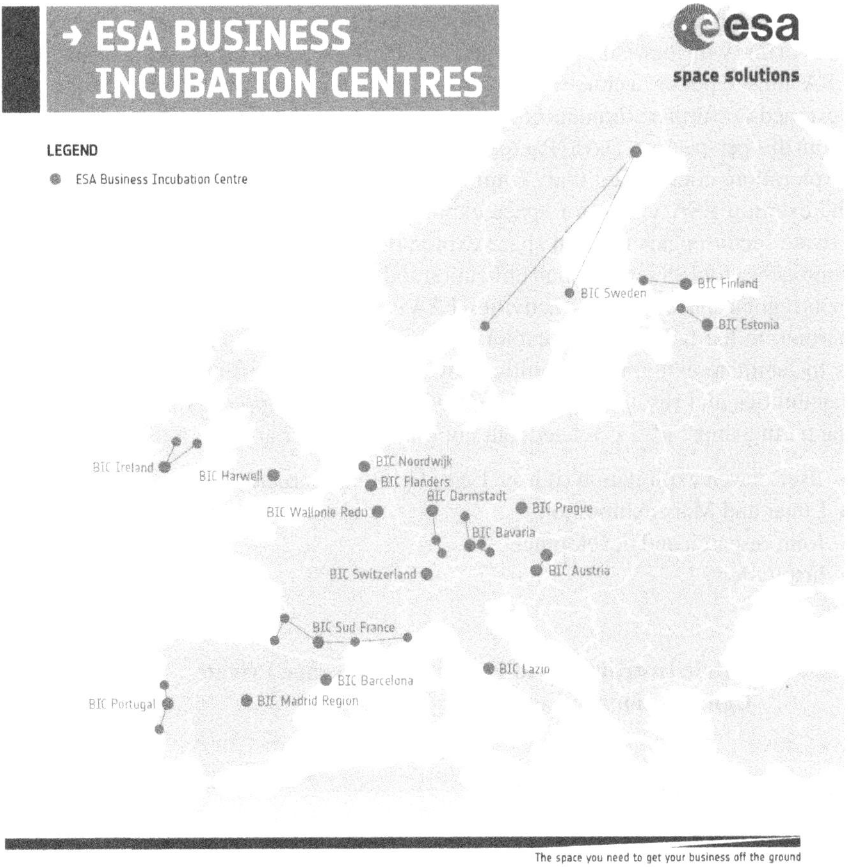

Fig. 3.3 Location of BICs in Europe. *Source* ESA [34]

space and non-space companies with the goal of enlarging the industrial base. ESA BICs help to create viable businesses and new jobs by providing support to over 100 companies every year around Europe [33]. The start-ups involved in the incubation centres generally address the downstream sector, with most of them focusing on developing new applications, but a growing number of endeavours, for example in Norway, Finland, Ireland or Switzerland also address the upstream space manufacturing sector.

Beyond ESA TTP and BICs, ESA is also investigating new ways to partner with the private sector to facilitate the realization of its ambitions in the space exploration sector.

In line with this strategic objective, ESA launched in 2015 a new mechanism known as Call for Ideas (CFI). This mechanism established a process for launching strategic partnerships with the private sector and positioning ESA as a business partner and sponsor of selected private sector initiatives. For the purpose of this CFI,

Table 3.3 Commercial partnerships status [36]

Objective	Partner	Partnership topic	MoU signed in
ISS exploitation	ADS—Bremen (D)	Optimization of ISS Utilization	–
	ADS—Bremen (D)	Bartolomeo—Commercial External Payload Service	May 2016
	SAS (B)	ICE Cubes	May 2016
	SAT4M2M (D)	TELDASAT	
Post-ISS LEO exploitation	OHB (D) Telespazio	Dream Chaser	June 2016
Lunar exploration	ADS—Bremen (D)	Commercial Moon Transport Capability	Feb. 2017
	SSTL Goonhilly	Lunar Communication System	June 2016
	PTScientists (D)	Lunar Surface Mission	–
R&D	OHB (D)	Environmental Simulation Chamber	–

"a Strategic Partnership is intended as a commitment between ESA and the private sector, including space and non-space industry, to short medium or longer-term relationships based on clear and mutually agreed objectives" [31]. Such partnerships also represent an opportunity for the private sector to shape and engage in the future global space exploration undertaking. The broader objectives of this initiative include fostering innovation, promoting innovative approaches into ESA space exploration missions and strengthening the competitiveness of European industry in providing exploration-enabling services [31]. The role pursued by ESA is to become a "business partner in developing new services or products on a non-exchange of funds principle, where the agency provides technical support and reviews, business development support, co-funds technology development and grants access to ESA facilities" [35].

Until February 2017, 9 out of 60 ideas received were selected for a pilot phase (Table 3.3). The topics covered include:

- Three commercial partnerships relate to the development and operations of private sector-owned ISS payload facilities
- One to promoting commercial utilization of existing Columbus payload facilities,
- One to the operations of a post-ISS infrastructure,
- Three to the provision of lunar exploration-related services,
- One for advancing ground-based R&D.

As shown in the table above, the range of ideas included applications, products and services related to utilization of the ISS, post-ISS LEO exploitation, lunar exploration, and ground analog tests. Fully in line with its Space Exploration Strategy, the agency aimed at promoting a broader utilization of the ISS, developing a step-wise approach to partner with private companies that would share risks.

Following the first success of the CFI, a permanent call has been established to continue receiving commercial partnership ideas. The new ideas that have undergone a successful consultation meeting undergo the same evaluation process during a pilot phase as the previous ideas currently developed. The commercial partnerships are now an integral part of E3P. In fact, the objectives of commercial exploration partnerships in E3P are [31]:

- Stimulate private participation in the space exploration framework,
- Foster innovative and inspiring approaches,
- Enhance private sector capabilities and demand for ISS utilization,
- Open perspectives for commercial approaches for exploitation of the ISS and post-ISS infrastructures.

After the adoption of the E3P, the agency is open to new business models with a commercial partner. Anyway, other different calls for proposals are established by ESA lately, such as in situ resource utilization (ISRU) in the framework of lunar missions and co-funded studies on platforms and facilities in LEO orbit in the framework of post-ISS [37].

Another objective of the agency is to explore and test innovative funding sources for space exploration, such as: "crowdfunding, sponsorship and prize schemes. Brainstorming activities with space and non-space actors are defining potential ways forward" [36]. In this frame, an upcoming event called ESA Grand Challenge, part of ESA's Space 4.0 Strategy, was recently proposed and approved by ESA Member States at the Council Meeting at Ministerial Level in December 2016. The ESA Grand Challenge has the central purpose to foster a new European ecosystem of entrepreneurs and start-up "competing to develop solutions that address complex problems be they technical, scientific or societal" [38].

The ESA Grand Challenge aims to create a new European ecosystem based on entrepreneurs and start-up companies, identifying new or unorthodox ideas, solutions or approaches to particular challenges. The purpose is to support cost-effective R&D, to foster innovation and entrepreneurship in space research and technology sectors, with the aim to use them for scientific purposes and for operational space applications systems [39]. However, this new tool may be used in the future to increase the research funds (the prize fund will originate from competitor's own investment and to reduce the risk of a public investment paying only case of success.

Recently, AZO Space of Innovation (Anwendungszentrum GmbH Oberpfaffenhofen, an international networking, and branding company for the European space programmes) on behalf of ESA has launched the Space Exploration Masters in line with ESA Space Exploration Strategy objectives. The Space Exploration Masters is an international competition to look for the best business idea, identifying the best technology transfer business successes and fostering exploration business innovation activities in LEO orbit, Moon, Mars and beyond. It is Europe's first innovation competition dedicated to space exploration that identifies the best transfer from the ESA Technology portfolio for space exploration to a non-space application.

The main focus of this innovation competition is to drive entrepreneurs and to become an important part of Europe's space exploration activities. There are two different prize categories "Technology Transfer Success" and "New Business Innovation" in the fields of human space and robotic missions, resources and industry, discovery and space observation, spacecraft, rockets, propulsion, space tourism, deep space communication and navigation, space habitats, and life sciences [40].

Regarding Technology Transfer Success Category, the main focus is to develop new solutions derived from non-space applications, into exploration activities, out of the ESA technology portfolio. The prize is about 10,000 € [41]. In the New Business Innovation Category, the value is around 500,000 € of in-kind prizes. The key objective of this competition is to develop new business innovations which are connecting space and non-space areas with new approaches and solutions in the space exploration framework.

European Union Support to Innovation and Competitiveness
The European Commission (EC) has set up a policy based on five priorities:

- Establish a coherent regulatory framework,
- Further develop a competitive, solid, efficient and balanced industrial base in Europe and support SME participation,
- Support the worldwide competitiveness of the European space industry and encourage the sector to become more cost-efficient along the value chain,
- Develop markets for space applications and services,
- Ensure the technological non-dependence and independent access to space.

In order to achieve the objectives of this policy in collaboration with ESA and the Member States, the EU can develop the framework conditions, using the instruments at its disposition and supporting research and innovation and promoting better use of financial instruments. In addition, EC pointed out, in the document *EU space industrial policy*, that research and innovation are considered not only the key elements of space industrial competitiveness but also for sustainable economic growth. The budget for space under Horizon 2020 is 1.737 million euro for 7 years. The programme covers R&D and innovation with the objectives to improve European competitiveness in space, focusing on industrial R&I and emphasizing SMEs; and enable European R&D in the context of international space partnerships (e.g. ISS, SSA, global robotic exploration programmes) [42].

The Commission aimed to organize regular dialogues with industry and other innovation actors, including the research community and users of applications and services, addressing their competitiveness needs. As stated in the document *Space Strategy for Europe* (2016), through the European Structural Investment Funds, the Commission has the objective to support the research and innovation Member States and regions, in this way the Commission will facilitate cross-border cooperation among their research and innovation actors. In addition, the Commission will foster closer cooperation with the European Institute of Innovation and Technology, and the main actions are [42]:

- Step up its efforts to support space R&D activities, in cooperation with Member States and ESA, and review its strategic approach to boosting the competitiveness of the European space sector,

- Strengthen the use of innovative procurement schemes to stimulate the demand-side of innovation and explore new approaches to leverage private sector investments and partnerships with industry,
- Promote the use of common technology roadmaps, together with Member States and ESA, ensuring complementarity of R&D projects,
- Engage in a dialogue with the EIB and EIF on the support of investment in space sector as part of the overall Investment Plan for Europe,
- Support space start-ups, exploring synergies with the upcoming Funds of Fund, and facilitate the emergence of space hubs and clusters in Europe.

The Commission's objective is to foster the space entrepreneurs and new business opportunities, promoting access to finance for space in the framework of the Investment Plan for Europe and Union funding programmes. In particular, the Investment Plan and the European Fund for Strategic Investments can play the role of supporting new and innovative projects. In addition, the Commission's intention is to engage in a dialogue with the European Investment Bank and European Investment Fund and explore synergies with the upcoming fund of funds [42].

Interestingly, the European Investment Fund operates as the investment arm of European Investment Bank, with the specialization in direct and fund of funds investments. In this way, for direct investments, the company seeks to invest in seed, growth, early stage and lower middle market investments. It makes fund of funds and equity investments in venture capital funds, private equity funds and business incubators that support the SMEs, start-ups and young entrepreneurs through business incubators and the use of prizes and competitions.

More importantly, the document, *Space Strategy for Europe* (2016), also highlighted that the emerge of a business and innovation ecosystem is supported at European, regional and national levels by establishing space hubs with the objective to open up space to non-space entrants through existing instruments within the Commission, ESA's business incubation centres and initiatives in the Member States (such as innovation cluster and boosters).

National Initiatives

At the national level, different programmes and mechanisms to foster innovation and to create a fertile ecosystem for the private sector are carrying out by the Member States. As already stated, space agencies in Europe are increasingly seeking to create new business opportunities and to stimulate new forms of public and private collaboration.

For example, in Germany, the DLR is trying to change the status quo by supporting different mechanism to engage private actors such as business incubation centres across Germany and running competitions that can offer support, including financial backing. One such initiative is named INNOspace Master; it is an annual competition that has the aim to activate young people to present their ideas to investors [43]. The winners will receive a certain amount of funding as mentoring from experts at DLR, ESA and Airbus, all of which support the individual INNOspace Masters Prizes.

In the space exploration framework, the Part-Time Scientists are a Berlin Germany based team of scientists and engineers with the goal to soft-land two lunar rovers. This

New Space company was one of the front runners in the Google XPRIZE and won two Milestone Prizes: the Mobility Prize ($500,000), and the Imaging Prize ($250,000) [44]. Its aim is to bring down the cost of space exploration and democratize access to the Moon. The company now relies on the support of AUDI AG and several other technology and research partners such as DLR.

In a comparable fashion, CNES President, Jean-Yves Le Gall, affirmed that "we don't perceive [New Space] as a threat but as a great opportunity that we intend to grasp with both hands" [45]. The agency is a driving force at the forefront of innovation with "several new generation projects" [45]. To provide the ground needed to seed development, the agency is stimulating the growth of a downstream ecosystem built around space technologies and infrastructures. Essentially, the ecosystem relies on a network of SMEs and mid-tier firms that are responding to a changing market, supported by stakeholders like CoSpace government industry space coordination committee, competitiveness clusters, incubators and accelerator, and public investment bank BPIfrance.

However, France intends to step up its research partnership efforts with France aerospace research agency ONERA and national scientific research centre, CNRS. In addition, CNES's new Directorate of Innovation, Application and Science (DIA) has a key role in shaping the agency's strategy. The general objective is to "*think outside the box*" [45] and to stimulate all initiatives for innovation and creative talent, creating synergies between the present and future users of space technologies.

In Italy, the President of ASI affirmed that a high proliferation of new actors in the space industry and how their activities are contributing to a transformation of the space sector. The President recalled the importance to understand how institutional budgets can be used and balanced in the evolving space economy. A recent decision by the Italian government confirmed the importance of complementarity between public and private funding, approving a 349M€ budget for a space economy plan and aiming to leverage 1.1B€ of private investments. In addition, the new ESA BIC Lazio, supported at the local level by the Lazio Region and by ASI, promotes technology transfer in Italy. Entrepreneurs and start-up companies can be hosted within the ITech Incubator at the Tecnopolo Tiburtino in Rome with the objective to support the development of innovative start-ups.

Finally, the UK Space Agency (UKSA) is also investing in new business incubators to boost the number of start-up companies in the UK. Recently, the agency has announced £200,000 of funding for four new business incubators with the aim to improve the economy and inspire the next generation of scientists and engineers. Business Secretary Greg Clark launched the Industrial Strategy to set out a long-term vision of how Britain can build on its economic strengths and support business and workers. This key policy embraces driving over £20 billion of investment in innovative and high potential businesses, establishing a new £2.5 bn Investment Fund, incubated in the British Business Bank [46].

3.3 Private Endeavours and Investment in Space Exploration

3.3.1 The Emergence of New Commercial Endeavours and Business Models

Involving highly complex systems, state-of-the-art technologies and requiring substantial investment, barriers to entry for business in the space sector have been high. Consequently, and with the noticeable exception of space launch services and satellite communication segments, space has been generally considered as an area not suitable for commercial ventures and investment from private actors in space has been, so far, limited.

This is evolving and a new generation of companies began to rise in the space sector. Today, new players are developing innovative business models based on new markets for space exploration and industrial activity. A number of entrepreneurs and new entrants have started new ventures to develop technologies and concepts to pursue a profitable business in the space exploration sector. Table 3.4 provides examples of this trend, including new companies and new business endeavours from already established players.

Those companies are structured around different business models and value propositions targeting a great variety of commercial objectives and markets. It is yet possible to group them into four main categories, described as follows:

- **Visionaries**: Companies targeting a very long-term and highly ambitious commercial objective in space exploration (e.g. mining of asteroids or celestial bodies, private settlements). These companies usually implement a step-wise approach based on an incremental technology development process,
- **Exploration Support Service Providers**: Companies offering commercial solutions that can support other private endeavours or be integrated into public exploration programmes (e.g. transportation, engineering, robotics, 3D printing, in-orbit servicing and assembly),
- **Business opportunity seekers**: Companies leveraging opportunities created by public space exploration programmes for purely commercial purposes (e.g. commercial utilization of the ISS),
- **Autonomous exploration-related businesses**: Companies whose business model is based on solutions developed independently from public institutions and addressing mainly commercial markets (e.g. private space stations for tourism). For these companies, public demand can be an important complement but does not constitute a pillar of business development.

The boundaries between each category are, of course, not always clear as the business model and commercial objective of some companies can correspond to more than one category. A list of representative examples is provided hereafter.

Table 3.4 Examples of new business endeavours in the space exploration domain

Company	Space exploration business	Latest developments
Argotec, Italy	Start-up offering multiple engineering and technical solutions for space systems with a focus on the ISS	• In 2010, Argotec was contracted by ESA as main food producer and supplier for European astronauts on the ISS
Deep Space Industries, USA/Luxembourg	Start-up developing technologies to facilitate access to deep space and exploit space resources	• DSI targeted to launch a private deep space mission in 2020 (Explorer spacecraft) • The start-up raised \$3.5M over 2 rounds • Plans were likely revised after DSI was acquired by Bradford Space in 2018 for an undisclosed amount
PTScientists, Germany	Start-up developing a spacecraft capable of delivering two rovers, or up to 100 kg of payload, to the lunar surface	• PTS signed a contract for ESA's planned in situ resource use (ISRU) mission and will provide the lunar lander that will analyse the regolith for future utilization
Space Adventures, USA	The first company providing opportunities for private astronauts to fly to and live in space	• In February 2019, the company signed a contract with the Russian Roscosmos for short-term flights to ISS of two unprofessional astronauts for 2021
SpaceIL, Israel	Start-up developing unmanned spacecraft on the Moon	• Founded in occasion of the Google Lunar XPRIZE in 2007 • In 2019, SpaceIL's lunar lander Beresheet was launched on board of a Falcon 9. It is the first-ever lunar private mission
Neora, Australia	Start-up seeking to be the world leader in the scanning and identification of asteroids	• Their innovative techniques will enable the use of the data to provide records of targets for asteroid mining
Goonhilly, UK	Start-up seeking to develop and expand Deep Space Communications	• In 2018, GES became part of the Commercial Lunar Mission Support Services. Currently upgrading Goonhilly, and developing small landers with a lunar mothership

(continued)

Table 3.4 (continued)

Company	Space exploration business	Latest developments
Planetary Resources, USA	Start-up enabling low-cost robotic exploration and commercial exploitation of asteroids	• In April 2018, the company launched Arkyd-6A (A6A), a technology demonstration to measure resources on water-rich asteroids
OffWorld, USA	Start-up developing a new generation of universal industrial robots for heavy lifting on Earth, Moon, asteroids and Mars	• OffWorld plans are to develop robots that would work under human supervision
Astrobotic, USA	Development of space robotic technology for lunar and planetary missions	• NASA awarded Astrobotics 2 contracts for developing technologies for the Peregrine Lunar Lander
Axiom Space, USA	Start-up manufacturing the first commercial space station. Axiom participated as TeamIndus to the Google Lunar XPRIZE	• After ISS retirement, Axiom Space has the willingness to help NASA to realize the transition from the ISS to the private one
Bigelow Aerospace, USA	Bigelow Aerospace design, build and construct habitable space structures	• In 2028, Bigelow announced the plan to launch and sell its own space station and created a spin-off company to manage and operate it
Moon Express, USA	Start-up providing lunar transportation and services for government and commercial customers	• In 2018, ME signed an MoU with the Canadian Space Agency to use Moon Express lunar orbiter and lander system for potential CSA payloads
Made In Space, USA	Start-up specializing in manufacturing and 3D printers for use in microgravity	• In 2018, Made In Space won a NASA contract to develop a hybrid material metal manufacturing system for space exploration, VULCAN
Airbus Defence and Space, Europe	Large Satellite Integrator	• In 2018, Airbus established a PPP with ESA to launch and operate Bartolomeo payload platform on the ISS • Airbus invested around €40 million • Additional payload resources will boost commercial exploitation of the ISS

(continued)

Table 3.4 (continued)

Company	Space exploration business	Latest developments
Space Application Services, Belgium/USA	Company offering space systems and software engineering solutions	• In 2017, SAS signed an agreement with ESA for the first commercial European opportunity to conduct research in space, ICE Cubes. The experiment price starts from €50,000 for 1 kg with cheaper rates for educational organizations

3.3.1.1 Selected Examples of Visionary Companies

Among the visionaries, companies like iSpace, Planetary Resources and Deep Space Industries best illustrate a new way of thinking big for commercial space exploitation in the long run.

iSpace Technologies Inc is a space resource exploration start-up with a vision to extend human presence beyond Earth and planning two lunar missions to orbit around and land on the Moon by 2020. Founded in 2013, their visionary value offer is to locate, extract and deliver lunar ice to customers in cis-lunar space. iSpace proposition comprises the developing microrobots thoroughly able to explore large areas of the Moon, at a fraction of the cost of large robots. The utilization of 3D printed and commercial off-the-shelf products (COTS) for rapid prototyping allowed a maximization in efficiency shortening the developmental life cycle. The start-up was born as the commercial evolution of the Google Lunar XPRIZE competition Team HAKUTO, one of the five final finalists and among the three teams to win a $500,000 Milestone Prize in mobility. In only three funding rounds, iSpace raised nearly $95 million and set a record in Japan. The two lead investors were Japan Airlines and Tokyo Broadcasting System. iSpace currently operates in Japan, Luxembourg and the USA, and has signed partnerships with JAXA and the government of Luxembourg. The Grand Duchy is among the main investors with a $28 million contribution, owing as a return the 10% share of the start-up.

A second traceable example is the US asteroid mining company **Planet Resources**. Founded in 2009 by Eric Anderson and Peter H. Diamandis, M.D. and acquired by ConsenSys on 31 October 2018, the company established a new paradigm for resource utilization envisioning low-cost robotic exploration and commercial exploitation of in situ resources. Asteroid mining is estimated to open access to a trillion-dollar industry and to provide a near-infinite supply of resources to support humanity's growth both on and off Earth. Currently, the basic value proposition of Planetary Resources is to identify and unlock the critical water resources necessary for human expansion in space. Their programme is an extensive data-gathering series of missions in deep space that will visit multiple near-Earth asteroids with the goal to answer the question of where we will establish the first mine in space and targeting both private and public actors as a customer. In April 2018, the company started its journey by launching Arkyd-6A (A6A), a technology demonstration to measure resources on water-rich asteroids. The company successfully lobbied towards the recognition of the right for US citizens to own asteroid resources, their exploitation and utilization. Planetary Resources announced a partnership with the government of Luxembourg to advance the industry in 2016. Not later than one year, the achievement of a Luxembourg's Chamber of Deputies law recognized the right to space-based resources. Despite having provided few details on how the mining would be carried out, a total of 24 among venture capital firms and business angels invested about $50,3 million in the company: OS Fund, Dylan Taylor, ZhenFund, Sinovation Ventures, Upslope Ventures, Sherpalo Ventures, Societe National de Credit et d'Investissement, among others.

Deep Space Industries (DSI) is another good example of the visionary category. DSI is a start-up founded to pursue the commercial goal of asteroid mining, it has been recently acquired by Bradford Space for an undisclosed amount. The US Bradford Space, owning facilities also in Netherland, Sweden and Luxembourg, is developing and building cost-efficient spacecraft technology that allows private companies and governmental agencies to access destinations throughout the solar system. Plans were likely revised after DSI was acquired by Bradford Space, but DSI's stated goal was to democratize access to deep space by fundamentally changing the paradigm for accessing deep space and substantially lowering the cost. DSI targeted to launch a private deep space mission in 2020, the Xplorer spacecraft, a versatile exploration spacecraft that can be used for a wide range of scientific and commercial missions in Earth orbit, and throughout the inner solar system. In two funding rounds, DSI raised $3.5M from business angel Eric Uhrhane and the venture capital firm Metatron Global.

3.3.1.2 Selected Examples of Exploration Support Providers

As commercial support service providers with already established customers (space agencies), PTScientists, Astrobotics, GoonHilly and OffWorld showcase well this emerging and most promising category of new ventures.

PTScientists is a German New Space start-up aiming to bring down the cost of space exploration. Established in 2010, PTS is committed to developing an affordable system to deliver experiments and payload to a targeted location. PTS recently signed a contract for ESA's planned in situ resource use (ISRU) mission and will provide the lunar lander that will conduct research over the regolith for its future utilization, highlighting PTS interdisciplinary innovation through the partnership with Audi (car manufacturer). Beaten on time by SpaceIL, the Berlin start-up planned to be the first private lunar mission.

Another relevant company populating the category of the exploration support providers is the US-based start-up **Astrobotics** created in 2007 in occasion of the Google Lunar XPRIZE and attained the finalist top 5. As a lunar logistic company, Astrobotics delivers payloads to the Moon opening his service to a various range of actors. Currently partnering with NASA through a Space Act Agreement under the Lunar CATALYST programme, the start-up has 30 prior and ongoing NASA contracts, in addition to 12 deals in place for its first mission and several customer negotiations for upcoming. The start-up's spacecraft accommodates manifold customers on a single flight, offering lunar delivery at an industry-defining price of $1.2 million per kilogram. Publically and privately invested, their latest funding has been raised on August 2018, reaching in total $12.5M thanks to a NASA grant, Space Angels and Dylan Taylor.

Goonhilly Earth Station (GES) Ltd is a private UK company owning and operating a ground station acquired back in 2014. GES is seeking to develop and expand Deep Space Communications and radio astronomy services. Currently, Goonhilly Earth Station is undergoing a sensitive technological upgrading. GES established the fastest commercial data connectivity system in the UK's southwest region and is currently launching the world's first commercial Deep Space Communications service. In 2018, Surrey Satellite Technology Limited (SSTL) and Goonhilly Earth Station (GES), in partnership with the European Space Agency (ESA), designed a set of Lunar Mission Support Services (LMSS) aiming to provide communications and operations services to support both orbiting and landed lunar assets. From 2014, GES announced two funding rounds from English investors for a total of €22.25 million from Downing LLP venture capital firm and the business angel Peter Hargreaves.

The **OffWorld** start-up is identified here as an exploration support provider due to his commitment to providing robotic components to in and out-of-space companies. Their exploration mission purpose can still be considered visionary despite not having yet proposed a concrete commercial offer. OffWorld plans to develop a new generation of industrial robots as a key enabler for human expansion beyond our planet. In pursuit of their aspirations, they are reinventing how they mine, process, manufacture and build cities on Earth.

3.3.1.3 Selected Examples of Business Opportunity Seekers

The business opportunity seeker category is best exemplified by companies involved in the commercial exploitation of the International Space Station including, for example, Airbus Defence and Space (Bartolomeo), Space Application Services or NanoRacks.

Bartolomeo is one of the newest solutions developed and commercialized by **Airbus Defence and Space**. Airbus is one of the most prominent space manufacturing primes in the international landscape. It has a portfolio of activities covering almost all space domains. Bartolomeo is a platform attached to the European Columbus module of the ISS and enabling the hosting of external payloads in Low Earth Orbit to serve a variety of applications including EO, robotics, material science and/or astrophysics; for institutional and private organizations alike. Bartolomeo platform is a highly cost and time-efficient *All-in-One Mission Service* comprises all mission elements into one commercial contract (mission preparation, payload launch, payload on-orbit installation, commissioning, operation, payload data processing and delivery), in order to provide the customer a reliable integrated mission solution. In order to develop this infrastructure, Airbus will invest €40 million within a commercial partnership (PPP) agreement framework for the construction, launch, and operations of this innovative platform, together with ESA providing Bartolomeo's installation on the ISS.

Under the same umbrella of the permanent open call to industry to participate in ESA's Space Exploration Strategy via innovative partnerships also the ICE Cubes project, presented by **Space Applications Services** NV/SA, Belgium, is currently operative on board of the Columbus module. The company is composed by a dynamic international group with 30 years' experience in performing and supporting system and software engineering throughout the complete project life cycle from establishing customer needs, designing and selecting the most appropriate technology, assembling the best team to implement the solution and, in some cases, operating the system for the customer. This service provides rapid and simplified access to the station on a commercial basis. For the first time, ICE Cubes offers room to run experiments and conduct research in weightlessness and to interact with the experiment directly from home. The price starts from €50,000 for a 1-kg experiment with an end-to-end service package running for four months, with cheaper rates for educational organizations.

Another company representing a good example for the category of the opportunity-seeking companies is **NanoRacks**. Since 2009, NanoRacks has truly created new markets and ushered in a new era of in-space services, dedicated to making space just another place to do business. NanoRacks Platforms embedded in the US National Lab is the ultimate "*Plug and Play*" commercial space research facility allowing small payloads to be plugged in, providing an interface with the Space Station power and data capabilities. Today, the company offers low-cost, high-quality solutions to the most pressing needs for satellite deployment, basic and educational research in over 30 nations worldwide increasing their customer log to over 50 customers, from high schools to universities, from pharmaceutical research organizations to non-ISS partners. By the end of 2017, NanoRacks announced the completion of its first external round of equity capital welcoming ten new angel and venture investors from both the US and Europe. Space Angels was the leading investor of this seed round providing early-stage funds. The undisclosed amount will be used for completing a commercial airlock module that NanoRacks plans to install on the ISS later in 2019.

3.3.1.4 Selected Examples of Exploration-Related Autonomous Businesses

Among autonomous exploration-related businesses, companies seeking to develop private space stations provide an interesting example. SpaceIL, who recently landed the first private spacecraft on the Moon, is also representative of this category of new ventures.

Bigelow Aerospace, established in 1999 by entrepreneur Robert T. Bigelow, an experienced developer, financier, buyer and manager of many large real estate projects in the USA provides an interesting showcase. Bigelow Aerospace is a research and development company focuses on achieving economic breakthroughs in the costs associated with the design, development and assembly of habitable space structures for private enterprise and government use. Bigelow has successfully launched in 2006 and 2007 two subscale spacecraft called Genesis I and II into orbit as well as the Bigelow Expandable Activity Module (BEAM), attached to the Tranquillity ISS module. Eventually, the last product on Bigelow portfolio is the B330 spacecraft a standalone habitat that can function autonomously for and beyond LEO destinations. Since 1999, Mr. Bigelow has personally provided all financial support totalling over $350 million to date.

An additional good example is represented by the Texas-based company **Axiom Space** founded in 2016 by CEO Michael T. Suffredini, former ISS programme manager at the NASA Johnson Space Center. The Axiom Space vision is to build the world's first commercial space station, stimulating a robust LEO economy and ensuring humanity's sustained research beyond LEO while enabling the permanence of government astronauts, private companies and individual explorers alike. The low-cost Low Earth Orbit platform access and decades of human spaceflight management experience support the research, testing of exploration-enabling technologies, and in-space manufacturing that will create new opportunities for advanced industries, governments, and educators and enable future human space exploration. The company has raised a small amount of money to support its operations until NASA awards a port on the ISS for its module. On the records are listed two deals, one of about $3 million raised at the very inception of the company itself and a second one of an undisclosed amount of money received in 2018. Once a port is awarded, the company will likely seek further investments to begin building the module itself.

Finally, the last example completing this showcase would be **SpaceIL** is a non-profit organization established in 2011, when three young engineers with the dream of landing the first Israeli spacecraft on the Moon entered the Google Lunar XPRIZE competition. In just three years, the organization has scaled into a national movement comprised of nearly twenty full-time staff, over 250 volunteers, and a network of hundreds of renowned academics, business leaders and industry experts. SpaceIL is actively working to create an Israeli "*Apollo Effect*" inspiring the next generation of young pupils to enrol in STEM. SpaceIL announced 24 February 2019 that its Beresheet lander performed its first manoeuver since being placed into a supersynchronous transfer orbit by a SpaceX Falcon 9. The spacecraft is scheduled to land on the Moon on 11 April. SpaceIL said the spacecraft was working well since launch, including successful deployment of its landing legs, with the exception of its star trackers. SpaceIL originally developed the lander as a one-off project to compete for the Google Lunar XPRIZE, with most of the $100 million cost of the project funded from philanthropic sources. The venture continued with the project even though Google terminated its sponsorship of the competition and funding of the prize purse a year ago. SpaceIL managed to successfully close a seed investment round in 2014 accounting of about $22.5 million from an international consortium of Adelson Family Foundation, Schusterman Foundation and Kahn Foundation.

3.3.2 *Evidence of a Growing Private Investment*

Beyond innovative approaches to public procurement introduced by space agencies, new companies, and business endeavours also leverage new sources of investment such as venture capital firms, business angels, private equity companies or banks, each with different investment mechanisms.

The growing number of private funding sources and the increasing size of investment in space start-ups is symptomatic of the new way the space sector and potential markets are considered with growing beliefs in opportunities for profitable business. Between 2000 and 2017, the cumulative investment (including debt financing) in start-up space ventures reached a total of $18.4 billion with strong growth over recent years [1] (Fig. 3.4).

Similar trends can be observed in Europe. Over the period 2014–2018, 113 private investment deals concerning European space start-ups were recorded for a total amount of €562.7 million. This value does not include investment in space ventures after they have successfully reached maturity. This concerns, among others, the acquisition of O3b Networks by SES or private placements in GOMspace after the initial public offering. Involving megadeals in the tens or hundreds of millions of euros, the total value of private investment in European space ventures, including mature ones, would reach €1,783.6 million on the period (Fig. 3.5).

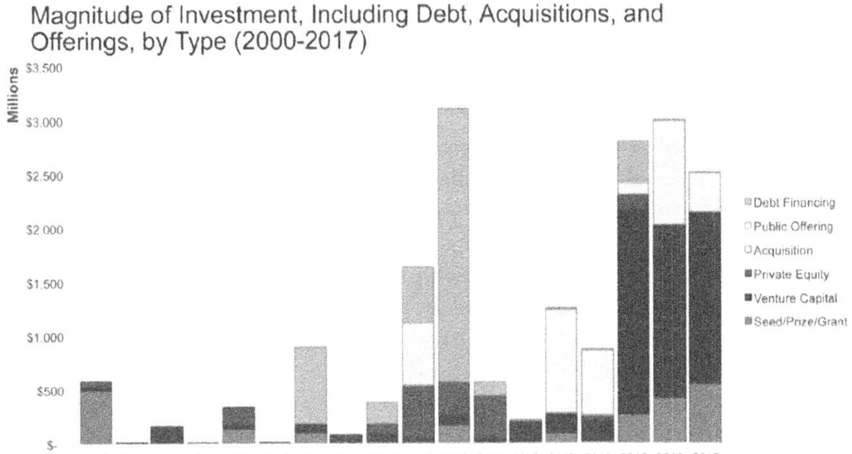

Fig. 3.4 Mix of types of investment in space companies varies from 2000 to 2017. *Source* Bryce [47]

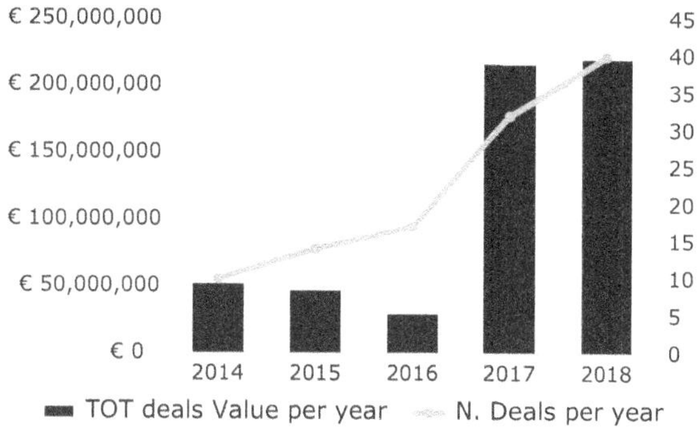

Fig. 3.5 Investment in European space start-ups (2014–2018) [48]

Although various studies have investigated investment trends in the space sector at large, a consolidated assessment of private investment in the space exploration domain has not yet been conducted. Notwithstanding, the multiplication of new business ventures, backed by substantial investments, suggests that space exploration and human spaceflight have also become domains of interest for private companies, entrepreneurs and investors, eager to engage in commercial endeavours and conduct business in these fields (Table 3.5).

These private investment operations come in addition to the private investment stimulated by innovative public instruments such as NASA COTS programme or ESA Strategic Partnerships.

In terms of investment size, venture capital (VC) firms and angel investors are the main sources of investment in the space sector. These two investor groups represent about 70% of the investment in space ventures. Private equity firms, corporations and banks make up for the remaining 30%. There is also small participation from a few foundations, who have contributed to grants and prizes, such as XPRIZE Foundation, Thiel Foundation, Knight Foundation and Space Frontier [47].

Since 2000, over 60 angel investors have financed the early stage of space companies. Business angel funds usually come from personal or corporate wealth [49]. The main characteristics can be summarized in three following concepts:

- Business angels invest in early-stage companies,
- The expected return is about 30–40% of their investments, and
- The time horizon of their funds varies from 5 to 7 years.

Principally, the Angels's activities are focused on New Space markets and distruptive solutions. This kind of investors can bring an attractive potential return, and this investment will secure an important foothold in the company. The most prominent angel investors are defined as "*space billionaires*". These billionaires have accrued their wealth through other successful businesses, founding either a space company or investing their own money in a space company. Concerning space exploration sector, Jeff Bezos (Blue Origin) and Elon Musk (SpaceX) are usually the first billionaires mentioned, but they are not the only ones. Other notable individual angel investors

Table 3.5 List of private investment deals in the space exploration domain (non-comprehensive)

Company	Investor	Value	Description
SpaceIL	Business angels • Adelson Family Foundation • Kahn Foundation • Schusterman Foundation	$22.4 million	Private investments from business angels complement public investments from the Israel Ministry of Science and Technology
Moon Express	venture capital firms and business angels • Minerva Capital Group • Other investors	$65.5 million	A total of 22 investors over six funding rounds. Minerva Capital Group is the leading investor with $12.5 million
NanoRacks	venture capital firms • Florida Space • Near Earth	$3.1 million	Public and private investments from a state-backed economic development agency and other undisclosed investors in NanoRacks' holding company XO Markets
Axiom Space (TeamIndus)	venture capital firms • Hemisphere Ventures • Starbridge venture capital • Balfour Capital	Undisclosed amount	Private investments in two rounds. The last funding was raised in January 2018
Astrobotic Technology	Business angels • Space Angels • Dylan Taylor	$12.5 million	Public and private investments over three different rounds
Planetary Resources	venture capital firms and Business angels • Tencent Holdings • Larry Page • Grishin Robotics • Peter Livingstong • Conversion Capital • Vast Ventures • OS Fund • Dylan Taylor • ZhenFund • Sinovation Ventures • Upslope Ventures • Sherpalo Ventures • Societe National de Credit et d'Investissement	$50.3 million	For a total of 24 investors, the last investments have been raised in 2016

(continued)

Table 3.5 (continued)

Company	Investor	Value	Description
Momentus Space	venture capital firms • Prime Movers Lab	\$8.3 million	By the end of 2018, Momentus raised a first seed round of private investments from a consortium of five micro-VC and one accelerator
Astroscale	venture capital firms • Innovation Network Corporation of Japan • Ana Holding	\$95 million	Astroscale has been particularly successful in raising money. Innovation NCJ has been the leading investor since 2016
Space Adventures	Business angel • Esther Dyson	Undisclosed	One round of private investment in 2008
Made In Space	venture capital firms • Space Angels • Starlight Ventures • Starbridge venture capital • Singularity University Venture	Undisclosed	Singularity University Venture invested in 2013 in the preseed round. The other three VC firms invested in 2018
GoonHilly	venture capital firms and business angels • Downing LLP • Peter Hargreaves	€26.7 million	Two funding rounds from English investors. The first has been announced in 2014 as a funding round from a VC firm while the second recorded in 2018 is from a business angel
Deep Space Industries	venture capital firms and business angels • Eric Uhrhane • Metatron Global	\$3.5 million	Recent Series A funding round to continue the ongoing development of its deep space exploration platform

in this sector are Larry Page (Planetary Resources) and Sheldon Adelson (SpaceIL) [47].

As is the case for the angels, the presence of VCs in the space market is increasing exponentially. They act in a different way from business angels: first, they are not single investors or wealthy families, but firms. This means that the level of risk that venture capitalists are ready to take is usually higher. Typically, VC funding has come in stages, designated as Series A, Series B and Series C, and they use the equity as a form of investment [1]. The stocks used by VCs give them an equity stake in the company they invest in with a higher level of priority than business angels, who are investors at common equity. Since 2000, over 110 VC firms have invested in early-stage space companies, for example, Moon Express, NanoRacks and Planetary Resources.

Other considerable private investment of space ventures that supports the start-up and scale-up phases are the corporations. Corporations have often provided the funding that is necessary to bring space-based programmes to initial operating capability, as well as to sustain ongoing programmes. In particular, corporations invest internally such as R&D, in manufacturing, in operations and processes and in other areas to enhance capabilities to create or strengthen existing expertise or advantage. Recently, the industry has seen a number of different investors in space. An example of a corporation serving as a strategic partner in space exploration is Tencent Holdings, an investment holding company based in China and that has invested in Moon Express and Planetary Resources [47].

An alternative approach that has been used in particular in the USA is competitive innovation prizes. These prizes are often financed by non-space actors, and it is utilized to mobilize resources and interest. The most high-profile prize is XPRIZE, in 2014, was the Ansari XPRIZE relating for Suborbital Spaceflight. The first part of the Ansari XPRIZE requirements was won $10 million by SpaceShipOne. This award was a major milestone in the development of private spaceflight capabilities [50]. A similar prize to Ansari XPRIZE was introduced in 2007: the Google Lunar XPRIZE. Its goal is to inspire a new generation of private investment in space exploration and technology.

Recently, in late 2017, several start-up space ventures will compete for the Google Lunar XPRIZE (GLXP). This year's Lunar XPRIZE contest sponsored by Google will likely kick off a new era in space-bound venture capital and entrepreneurship [51].

The GLXP competition will award $20 million to the first privately funded team that notifies XPRIZE about its launch and landing site; safely lands a craft with a GLXP (specified payload on the Moon); navigates its craft at least 500 m above or under the lunar surface; transmits two "Mooncasts"; and transmits and retransmits data provided by XPRIZE. The second team will receive a $5 million award. On December 2017, Team Indus has raised over $35 million since 2014 and plans to launch its spacecraft to the Moon on board a PSLV (December 2017) which the goal of landing on the lunar surface in late January 2018. Moon Express has received over $50 million of an angel, venture and private equity investment since 2011 and has selected Rocket Lab, another start-up space company, to launch its spacecraft on board the Electron launch vehicle. However, Moon Express has also announced plans to launch several missions to the lunar surface after the GLXP competition, including resource prospecting and sample return missions [47].

Finally, another interesting mechanism is crowdfunding. This initiative offers space organizations avenues for fundraising outside traditional institutional methods. It is a method for individual citizens to pool their resources, usually via the Internet, to support efforts initiated by other people or organizations. In addition to

Table 3.6 Thousands of people have directly contributed to developing space projects by donating funds

Year	Company	Funding goal	Platform
2011	KickSat	$30,000	Kickstarter
2012	ArduSat	$35,000	Kickstarter
2012	Uwingu	$75,000	Indiegogo
2012	STAR Systems	$20,000	Kickstarter
2012	LiftPort Group	$8,000	Kickstarter
2012	Hyper-V	$69,000	Kickstarter
2013	Aerospace Industries Association	$33,000	Indiegogo
2013	Lunar Orbiter Image Recovery Project	$75,000	RocketHub
2013	Planetary Resources	$1M	Kickstarter
2014	Skycorp/SpaceRef/Space College	$125K	RocketHub

Source NASA [50]

providing crucial funds for the companies, crowdfunding allows citizens to directly engage in space exploration by funding the projects that interest them. Sites like *Kickstarter.com, Rockethub.com and Indiegogo.com* allow space companies to tap the financial resources of private citizens interested in space exploration. For example, the ISEE-3 programme, a NASA probe launched in 1978, became the first spacecraft in deep space to be operated by a private sector organization thanks in part to RocketHub (a crowdfunding company) (Table 3.6).

References

1. A. Vernile, *The Rise of Private Actors in the Space Sector* (Springer, ESPI, 2017)
2. NASA, *Commercial Orbital Transportation Services a New Era in Spaceflight* (2014). Retrieved from: https://www.nasa.gov/sites/default/files/files/SP-2014-617.pdf
3. NASA, *The Vision for Space Exploration* (2004). Retrieved from https://history.nasa.gov/Vision_For_Space_Exploration.pdf
4. D. Mosher, *Russia is Squeezing NASA for More than $3.3 billion—And There's Little Anyone Can Do About It* (2016). Retrieved from Business Insider: http://www.businessinsider.de/astronaut-cost-per-soyuz-seat-2016-9?r=U.S.&IR=T
5. S.3729—111th Congress, *National Aeronautics and Space Administration Authorization Act of 2010* (2009–2010). Retrieved from Congress.Gov: https://www.congress.gov/bill/111th-congress/senate-bill/3729
6. Space News Staff, *BREAKING|President Trump reestablishes National Space Council* (2017). Retrieved from Space News: http://spacenews.com/breaking-president-trump-reestablishes-national-space-council/
7. C. Davenport, *Donald Trump Planning to Turn International Space Station into Commercially-Run Property Venture* (2018). Retrieved from Independent: https://www.independent.co.uk/news/world/americas/us-politics/donald-trump-international-space-station-iss-nasa-commercial-venture-federal-funding-ends-2024-space-a8206046.html

8. NASA, *NASA Strategic Plan 2018* (2018). Retrieved from https://www.nasa.gov/sites/default/files/atoms/files/nasa_2018_strategic_plan.pdf
9. M. Wall, *Trump's 2019 NASA Budget Request Puts Moon Ahead of Space Station* (2018). Retrieved from Space.com: https://www.space.com/39671-trump-nasa-budget-2019-funds-moon-over-iss.html
10. NASA, *FY 2019, Budget Estimates* (2019). Retrieved from https://www.nasa.gov/sites/default/files/atoms/files/nasa_fy_2019_budget_overview.pdf
11. K. Leary, *Trump Wants to Put the ISS in the Hands of Private Industry* (2018). Retrieved from Futurism: https://www.washingtonpost.com/news/the-switch/wp/2018/02/11/the-trump-administration-wants-to-turn-the-international-space-station-into-a-commercially-run-venture/?utm_term=.9d8533cba50a
12. NASA, *International Space Station Transition Report Pursuant to Section 303(c) (2) of the NASA Transition Authorization Act of 2017 (P.L. 115-10)* (2018). Retrieved from https://www.nasa.gov/sites/default/files/atoms/files/iss_transition_report_180330.pdf
13. D. Messier, *NASA's ISS Transition Report* (2018). Retrieved from Parabolic Arc: http://www.parabolicarc.com/2018/05/21/iss-transition/
14. The National Academy Press. *Technical Analysis and Affordability Assessment of Human Exploration Pathways*. Retrieved from https://www.nap.edu/read/18801/chapter/6
15. J. Hampson, *The Future of Space Commercialization* (2017). Security Studies, The Niskanen Center: https://science.house.gov/sites/republicans.science.house.gov/files/documents/TheFutureofSpaceCommercializationFinal.pdf, https://science.house.gov/sites/republicans.science.house.gov/files/documents/TheFutureofSpaceCommercializationFinal.pdf
16. R.J. Pielke, B. Radford, *Shuttle Programme Lifetime Cost* (2011). Retrieved from International Journal of Science: https://www.nature.com/articles/472038d#/author-information
17. C.L. Meehan, *Fixed Price Vs. Cost Plus*. Retrieved from http://smallbusiness.chron.com/fixed-price-vs-cost-plus-2220.html
18. E. Berger, *Elon Musk Knows What's Ailing NASA—Costly Contracting* (2017). Retrieved from ArsTEchinica: https://arstechnica.com/science/2017/07/elon-musk-knows-whats-ailing-nasa-costly-contracting/
19. NASA, *Commercial Orbital Transportation Services Report* (2014). Retrieved from https://www.nasa.gov/sites/default/files/files/SP-2014-617.pdf
20. NASA, *National Aeronautics and Space Act of 1958, As Amended* (1958). Retrieved from https://history.nasa.gov/spaceact-legishistory.pdf
21. M. Mazzucato, R. Douglas, *Lost in Space? NASA and the Changing Public-Private Ecosystem in Space*. Working Paper Series (SWPS) 2016–2020 (SPRU, University of Sussex, 2016) (Science Policy Research Unit)
22. G. Martin, *NewSpace: The Emerging Commercial Space Industry ISU MSS 2017* (2017). Retrieved from NASA: https://ntrs.nasa.gov/archive/nasa/casi.ntrs.nasa.gov/20170001766.pdf
23. NASA, *AES Overview*. Retrieved from NASA: https://www.nasa.gov/content/aes-overview
24. NASA, *Innovative Partnerships with AES*. Retrieved from NASA: https://www.nasa.gov/content/aes-partnerships
25. NASA, *Lunar CATALYST.* Retrieved from NASA: https://www.nasa.gov/lunarcatalyst
26. J. Foust, *NASA Will Pay More for Less ISS Cargo Under New Commercial Contract* (2018). Retrieved from Space News: http://spacenews.com/nasa-will-pay-more-for-less-iss-cargo-under-new-commercial-contracts/
27. NASA, *NASA Selects Six Companies to Develop Prototypes, Concepts for Deep Space Habitats* (2016). Retrieved from NASA: https://www.nasa.gov/press-release/nasa-selects-six-companies-to-develop-prototypes-concepts-for-deep-space-habitats
28. J. Foust, *NASA Seeks Information on Developing Deep Space Gateway Module* (2017). Retrieved from Space News: http://spacenews.com/nasa-seeks-information-on-developing-deep-space-gateway-module/
29. J. Foust, *NASA Issues Study Contracts for Deep Space Gateway Element* (2017). Retrieved from Space News: http://spacenews.com/nasa-issues-study-contracts-for-deep-space-gateway-element/

30. ESA. *ESA Council Meeting Held at Ministerial Level on 1 and 2 December 2016 Resolutions and Main Decisions* (2016). Retrieved from ESA: http://esamultimedia.esa.int/docs/corporate/For_Public_Release_CM-16_Resolutions_and_Decisions.pdf
31. ESA, *Call for Ideas. Space Exploration as a Driver for Growth and Competitiveness: Opportunities for the Private Sector* (2016). Retrieved from: http://emits.sso.esa.int/emits-doc/ESTEC/ESA-Call-for-Ideas-Space-Exploration.pdf
32. ESPI, *Autumn Conference 2016*. Outcome Report (2017)
33. ESA, *ESA Business Incubation Centers*. Retrieved from: http://www.esa.int/Our_Activities/Space_Engineering_Technology/Business_Incubation/ESA_Business_Incubation_Centres12
34. ESA, *ESA Business Incubation Centers*. Retrieved from ESA: http://www.esa.int/spaceinimages/Images/2016/03/ESA_Business_Incubation_Centres_-_September_2017
35. B. Hufenbach, *Astronautics Engaging the Private Sector in Space Exploration* (2017). Retrieved from Room the Space Journal: https://room.eu.com/article/engaging-the-private-sector-in-space-exploration
36. B. Hufenbach, L. Borggräfe, L. Summerer, E. Sourgens, L. del Montee, V. La Regina, *Engaging the Private Sector in Space Exploration—An ESA Approach* (2016). Retrieved from https://www.esa.int/gsp/ACT/doc/CMS/pub/ACT-RPR-1610-IACEngagingPrivateSectorExploration.pdf
37. ESA, *Partners for Space Exploration*. Retrieved from ESA: http://www.esa.int/About_Us/Business_with_ESA/Business_Opportunities/Partners_for_Space_Exploration/(print)b
38. ESA, *Global Space Economy Forum: Community of Innovation*. Retrieved from ESA: http://www.esa.int/About_Us/Business_with_ESA/Global_Space_Economic_Forum/Global_Space_Economic_Forum_Community_of_Innovation
39. ESA, *ESA Grand Challenge Statutes* (2016). Retrieved from http://esamultimedia.esa.int/docs/corporate/ESA_Grand_Challenge.pdf
40. ESA, *Space Exploration Open for Business* (2017). Retrieved from ESA: http://www.esa.int/About_Us/Business_with_ESA/Business_Opportunities/Space_exploration_open_for_business
41. Space Exploration Masters. The Results, 2017. Initiated by ESA and organized by AZO. Space of Innovation. Retrieved from: http://www.asi.it/sites/default/files/attach/notizia/spaceex_flyer_general_2017-web.pdf
42. European Commission, *Communication from the Commission to the European Parliament, the Council, the European Economic and Social Committee and the Committee of the Regions Eu Space Industrial Policy* (2016). Retrieved from http://eur-lex.europa.eu/LexUriServ/LexUriServ.do?uri=COM:2013:0108:FIN:EN:PDF
43. T. Pultarova, *Germany Wants More Space Startups But Entrepreneurs Struggle for Liftoff* (2017). Retrieved from Space News: http://spacenews.com/germany-wants-more-space-startups-but-entrepreneurs-struggle-for-liftoff/43
44. Google Lunar XPRIZE, *Team Part-Time Scientists*. Retrieved from Google Lunar XPRIZE: https://lunar.xprize.org/teams/part-time-scientists
45. CNES, *Inventing the Future of Space*. Retrieved from https://cnes.fr/sites/default/files/drupal/201701/default/is_presentation_corporate_2017_en.pdf
46. Gov.UK, *New Business Incubators Will Help Space Industry Grow* (2017). Retrieved from Gov. UK: https://www.gov.uk/government/news/new-business-incubators-will-help-space-industry-grow
47. Bryce. Space and Technology, *Start-Up Space Update on Investment in Commercial Space Ventures* (2018). Retrieved from https://brycetech.com/downloads/Bryce_Start_Up_Space_2018.pdf
48. ESPI, *Space Ventures Europe 2018*
49. S.G. Morrissette, *A Profile of Angel Investors* (2007). College of Business at University of St. Francis injoliet. Retrieved from https://eclass.aueb.gr/modules/document/file.php/LOXR116/02%20Venture%20Capital/Articles/Morrissette_(07)_JPE.pdf
50. NASA, *Emerging Space the Evolving Landscape of 21st Century American Spaceflight* (2014). Retrieved from https://www.nasa.gov/sites/default/files/files/Emerging_Space_Report.pdf

51. G. Reback, *Forget SpaceX: 10 Companies that will Change Space Travel in 2017 & 2018* (2017). Retrieved from https://www.geektime.com/2017/03/01/forget-spacex-10-companies-that-will-change-space-travel-in-2017-2018/

Chapter 4
Commercial Contributions and Public–Private Partnerships

4.1 Key Public–Private Partnership Concepts

4.1.1 Models

The public–private partnership (PPP) model is one of the most common tools to formalize relations between private actors and the public sector. There is no single or simple definition of PPP since the term covers a range of different types of contracts or other delivery models. The term PPP is used for any form of association or cooperation between the public and private sectors for the purpose of delivering a project or service. According to the OECD, a public–private partnership can be defined as "an agreement between the government and one or more private partners (which may include the operators and the financers) according to which the private partners deliver the service in such a manner that the service delivery objectives of the government are aligned with the profit objectives of the private partners and where the effectiveness of the alignment depends on a sufficient transfer of risk to the private partners [1]".

Throughout the project, partners share responsibilities over the different phases and resources mobilized to conduct the programme: finance, design, build and operate. Generally, as represented in Fig. 4.1, the different PPP models can be characterized according to the level of responsibility of public and private partners.

PPP schemes are structured according to how responsibilities are shared between the partners throughout the different phases of the project. Responsibilities include resources mobilization, the conduct of operations, ownership of assets and, in general, liability over project risks. To select an appropriate PPP scheme, the level of responsibilities should take into account the level of benefits (e.g. for private entities: profits, competitiveness, access to new markets/for public entities: reduction of costs, improved services, support to industrial base) that will arise for each actor from the PPP. In particular, the involvement of private funding must be motivated by some

C. Iacomino, *Commercial Space Exploration*,
SpringerBriefs from the European Space Policy Institute,
https://doi.org/10.1007/978-3-030-15751-7_4

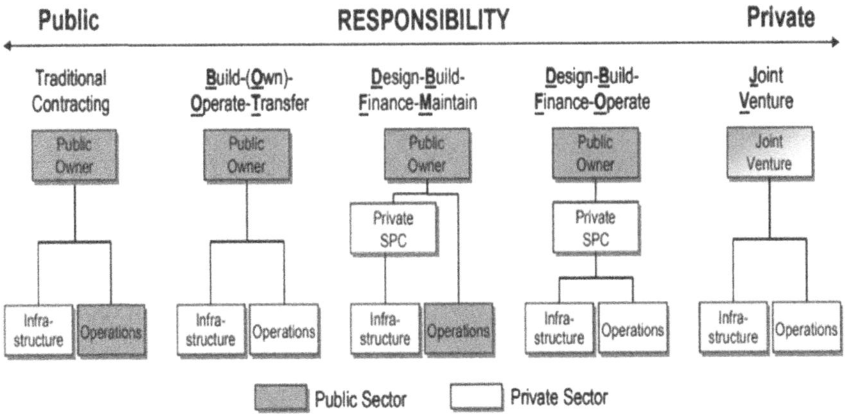

Fig. 4.1 PPP types and responsibility transfer [2]

return on investment, either through revenues covering the investment or other direct and indirect benefits [2].

From the public perspective, the first criterion to determine the most appropriate PPP scheme for a project is to compare the potential benefits of the arrangement to resources required to implement it. Other criteria must also be taken into account to validate the suitability of a PPP scheme, including project characteristics and partners' objectives and requirements including, on the private side, the business rationale. In general, the following factors can be taken into account [3]:

- **Project size**: In general, larger projects may have more opportunities to create PPP value (and offset the higher transaction costs).
- **Project duration**: Projects with longer life cycles are often more suited for PPPs. However, many smaller PPP projects can have shorter durations.
- **Project complexity**: More complex projects have more opportunities for private sector innovation.
- **Public alternative**: If the government is unable to provide the infrastructure or service itself (for capacity, technical, financial or other reasons), then a PPP may be the only option.
- **Potential market interest**: Private companies have interest and capacity to develop a profitable business case for the project.
- **Legacy**: If other projects for the same or very similar infrastructure or service have been done before on a PPP basis.
- **Potential lifecycle integration**: Projects which can allow the private partner to deal with the infrastructure design, provision, operation and maintenance are more suited for PPPs.
- **Potential commercial exploitation**: Projects which have the potential for the generation of other sources of income have more potential as PPPs.

4.1.2 Structure and Contractual Relationships

The structure of a PPP can be quite complex involving contractual arrangements between a number of parties including the government, project sponsor, project operator, financiers, suppliers, contractors, engineers, third parties and customers. The actual structure of a PPP depends on the type of partnerships [4].

In general, PPP can be grouped into three categories legal structures and arrangements. First of all, it can be used to introduce private sector ownership into state-owned business through the introduction of an equity partner. Secondly, it can introduce a public partner into a private initiative where the government supports the initiative in an exchange for specific benefits. Thirdly, it can involve the selling of government services or infrastructures to private partners, or vice versa, to better exploit their commercial potential.[1]

In these three arrangements, the private actors typically form a consortium called special-purpose vehicle (SPV), with the aim to develop and manage the project. The SPV is a "legal entity that undertakes a project. All contractual agreements between the various parties are negotiated between themselves and the SPV. An SPV is a commercial company established under the relevant Act of a country through an agreement (also known as a memorandum of association) between the shareholders or sponsors. The shareholders' agreement sets out the basis on which a company is established, giving such details as its name, ownership structure, management control and corporate matters, authorized share capital and the extent of the liabilities of its members" [5]. Within the PPP, it is the SPV that signs the contract with the government and with subcontractors to build the facility and then maintain it.

As shown in Fig. 4.2, the SPV raises finance through a combination of equity (provided by the project company's shareholders) and debt provided by banks, or other financial instruments. The finance structure is the combination of equity and debt, and contractual relationships between the equity holders and lenders.

Generally, the SPV may enter into a single contract with a group of companies that will divide the works among themselves. Alternatively, the SPV may enter into separate contracts with different groups of contractors for the specific elements. In particular, most of the rights and obligations will be transferred to a downstream structure that includes contracts, allocation responsibilities, obligations and risks and cash flows from the SPV to the different private actors through different agreements [6]:

- Shareholders agreements (especially with financial investors),
- Financial or debt agreements,
- Construction/engineering, procurement and construction (EPC) contracts,
- O&M contract or contracts,
- Insurance contracts and guarantees.

[1] "A franchise is a type of license that a party (franchisee) acquires to allow them to have access to a business's (the franchiser) proprietary knowledge, processes, and trademarks in order to allow the party to sell a product or provide a service under the business's name".

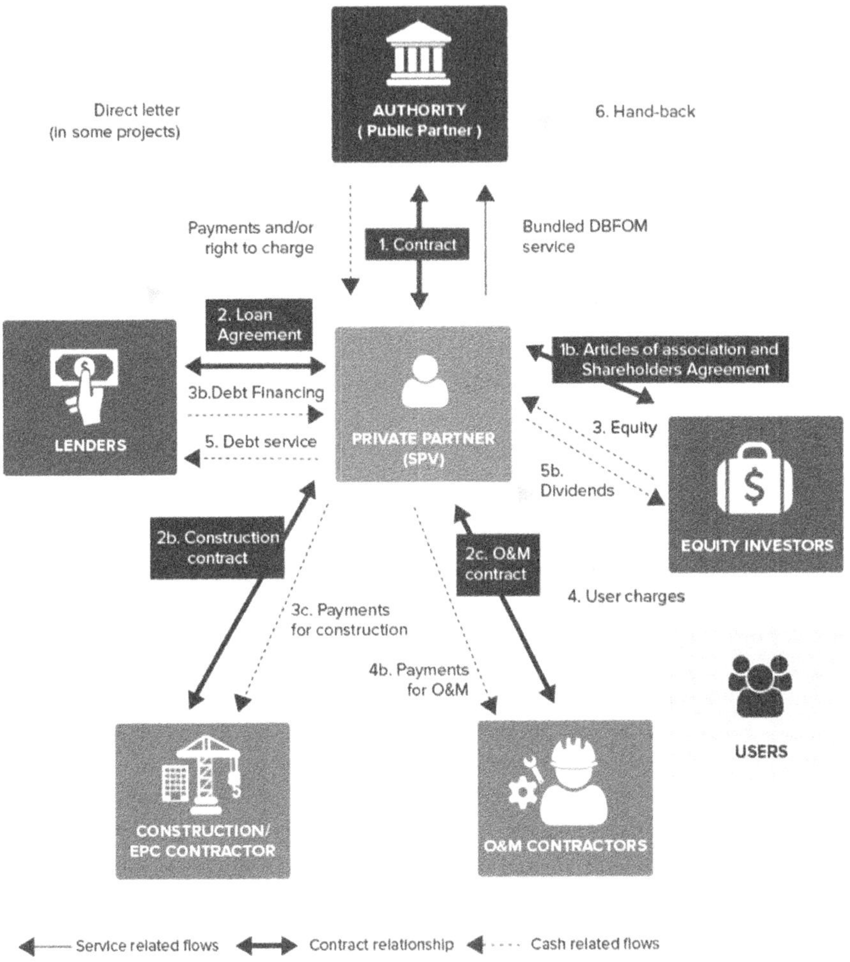

Fig. 4.2 Typical structure of a PPP project [6]

With regard to the project, the SPV can assume the following responsibilities [6]:

- **To design** the infrastructure or service according to the requirements of the partners,
- **To build** the infrastructure or develop the service (including obtaining all permits necessary if obliged to do so),
- **To finance** the works and other development costs (the full costs, or a relevant portion if the contract has a co-finance structure with grant financing from the government),
- **To operate** and maintain the infrastructure or deliver the service (after commissioning the asset and obtaining approvals and authorizations).

4.1.3 Risk Management

From a general standpoint, risk is defined as the "uncertainty of outcome, whether positive opportunity or negative threat, of actions and events" [7]. The level of risk is characterized by two factors: the likelihood of the event taking place and the impact of the event [7]:

- **The likelihood**: the probability of the risk event occurring within the time period of the project,
- **The impact**: the financial value of the risk event's effect.

More specifically, in a project, risk can be defined as an uncertain event that, if it occurs, has a negative effect on the project's objectives. While under traditional procurement, the public sector retains a significant share of the risks, a key component of PPP procurement involves the transfer of some risks from the public sector to the private sector. Risk transfer is a "risk management and control strategy that involves the contractual shifting of a pure risk from one party to another" [8].

Risk management in a project follows a cycle which, in sequence, includes: risk identification, risk assessment, preliminary allocation, (early) risk mitigation, risk allocation and risk structuring. Through this process, some risks are transferred to the private partner, some risks are retained by the public partner, and some risks are shared.

Identification of risks involves a comprehensive review of risk events, usually grouped in consistent categories, and described so as to understand clearly how those risks will impact the project outcome if they materialize. It is a common and good practice to use a "risk matrix". A risk matrix identifies and systematically describes all risks properly, including how they affect the project, as well as potential mitigation measures (a risk may potentially have a severe impact, but be easy to mitigate). The risk matrix helps the partners to organize the risk analysis and allocation. The decision will usually be made by means of qualitative assessment.

The main types of business risk can be catalogued in the following categories [9]:

- **Construction risk**: This is the possibility that during the construction phase the project costs or construction time exceeds those projected. In practice, it is related to events such as late delivery, non-respect of specified standards, significant additional costs, legal and environmental issues, technical deficiency and external negative effects (including environmental risk) triggering compensation payments to third parties.
- **Availability and quality risk (and revenue risk from the private perspective)**: This risk refers to the risk (especially from the public perspective) of the infrastructure not being available to use and or not meeting the quality or expected performance levels and covers cases where, during the operation of the asset, the responsibility of the partner is called upon, because of insufficient management ("bad performance"), resulting in a volume of services lower than what was contractually agreed, or in services not meeting the quality standards specified in the contract.

- **Demand risk**: It covers the variability of demand (higher or lower than expected when the contract was signed) irrespective of the performance of the private partner. In other words, a shift of demand cannot be directly linked to inadequate quality of the services provided by the partner. However, the quantitative and qualitative shortfalls have an impact on the effective use of the service and in some cases exert an eviction effect, but this primarily results from bad management of the availability risk. Instead, it should result from other factors, such as the business cycle, new market trends, a change in final users' preferences or technological obsolescence. This is part of a usual "economic risk" borne by private entities in a market economy.
- **Financial risk**: Most categories of risk have a financial impact, in terms of extra costs or lost revenue. But the category of financial risk refers specifically to the money flowing in and out of your business, and the possibility of a sudden financial loss.
- **Operational risk**: Risk refers to an unexpected failure in your company's day-to-day operations. It could be a technical failure, as a server outage, or it could be caused by your people or processes. In some cases, operational risk has more than one cause.

Once risks are allocated and structured, an effective management strategy will be implemented. The partners will structure and develop a specific management strategy for each risk. These strategies typically include [7]:

- Self-insuring and building up contingency funds in the budget,
- Contracting out insurance policies for some risks,
- Entering into hedging mechanisms for some financial or economic risks (e.g. inflation),
- Relying only on reactive management when a particular risk occurs, and
- For all risks, the public partner will design and operate a risk monitoring system which will incorporate mechanisms to review the identified risks, detect new risks as they arise, and establish how to deal with the risks when they occur, including risks that have been transferred. The public partner monitors both retained and transferred risks because it has the ultimate responsibility to the taxpayer for the asset and the service it provides.

Projects with long life cycles can be subject to a high number of risks that even the most careful set of provisions and remedies can fail to consider.

The objective of the risk transfer is to achieve an optimal risk allocation. The risks should be allocated to the party best able to manage them. In other words, the party that is best able to understand the risk, control the likelihood of the risk occurring and/or minimize the impact of the risk should also be responsible for managing it [10, see also 11].

The *effective* allocation of risk has a direct impact on the financial structure of the project where the risk allocation is critical for the success of the project. The degree of risk transfer to the private sector will influence the overall cost of the project to the public sector, as risk will be associated with a price premium.

Table 4.1 Effective risk transfer of PPP delivery method [12]

Risk	Type of project			
	Traditional contracting		PPP	
	Public	Private	Public	Private
Design risks	X			X
Construction risks		X		X
Entitlements and utilities	X			X
Completion risk	X			X
Disputes between designer and builder	X		X	X
Landlord risk and shortfalls	X			X
Operation and maintenance	X			X
Regulatory compliance	X			X
Capital maintenance	X			X
Technological obsolescence	X			X
Excess energy consumption	X			X
Environmental regulations	X		X	X
Changes in law	X		X	
Force majeure events	X		X	
Pre-existing conditions	X		X	X
Commissioning delays	X		X	X
Inflation	X		X	

Table 4.1 shows how risk is transferred to private partners between a traditional contracting approach and a more ambitious PPP scheme.

4.1.4 Value for Money

Public entities may pursue PPP schemes for a variety of reasons, including access to private capital, improved budget certainty, accelerated project delivery, transfer of risk to the private sector, the attraction of private sector innovation and improved or more reliable levels of service. The involvement of the private funding in public projects is to increase the effectiveness, allowing the public sector to cope with lack of immediate funds by translating up-front capital into a flow of ongoing service payments and potential grants.

In particular, one of the key motivations for governments to procure and deliver projects via PPP models is the assumption that PPPs may, in specific situations, deliver a higher value for money (VfM). VfM is defined as "the utility that a customer derives from the product/service in return for the economy (money) spent on it. It is a measure of the effectiveness and/or the efficiency of the product. It is an

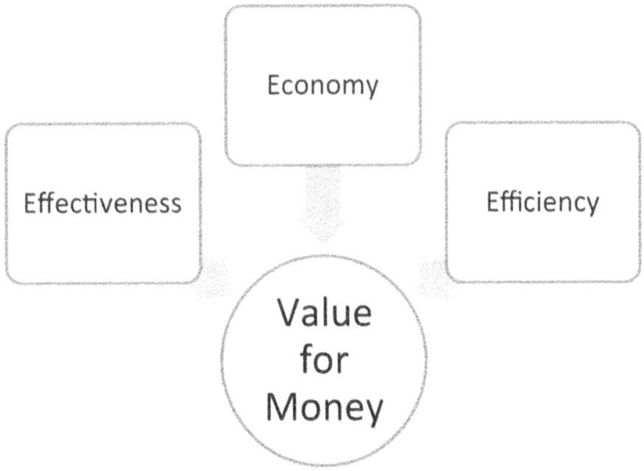

Fig. 4.3 Efficiency, effectiveness and economy [15]

assessment as to whether the customer has derived the maximum benefit possible from the good/service, within the constraints of the resources (time, money, materials) available" [13].

The VfM analysis considers the optimum combination of lifecycle costs and quality. The VfM analysis process is used on a case-by-case basis to compare the aggregate benefits and costs of a PPP procurement against those of the conventional public alternative. This means delivering a project with the same quality as under traditional procurement for less money or delivering a project with superior quality and innovation for the same amount of money [13]. The VfM analysis then seeks the right balance between economy (i.e. savings), efficiency and effectiveness, interrelated factors that cannot be assessed in isolation (Fig. 4.3) [14, see also 15]:

- **Economy** (reducing costs of inputs): reducing the cost of resources used for an activity, for maintaining quality,
- **Efficiency** (the right effort allocation): increasing output for a given input, or minimizing input for a given output, for maintaining quality,
- **Effectiveness** (to achieve the goals): successfully achieving the intended outcomes from an activity.

Another aspect is that the VfM analysis can be used to select a project´s preferred procurement option such as traditional procurement or PPP and to identify and negotiate the selected bidder prior to finalizing the PPP agreement. For each procurement approach, the VfM process establishes an overall evaluation of the cost estimated for the sum of all project elements, including costs of risks. This includes not only a project's construction or capital expenditures (CAPEX), but also the ongoing costs that a company pays to run its basic business, such as costs associated with operating and maintaining it (OPEX). There are also included procurement costs and the costs for project development. The sum of these cots is referred to as a project´s lifecycle cost.

The optimal risk allocation is one of the key VfM drivers in a PPP delivery model. VfM is achieved when a PPP project is able to generate: cost-effectiveness, through

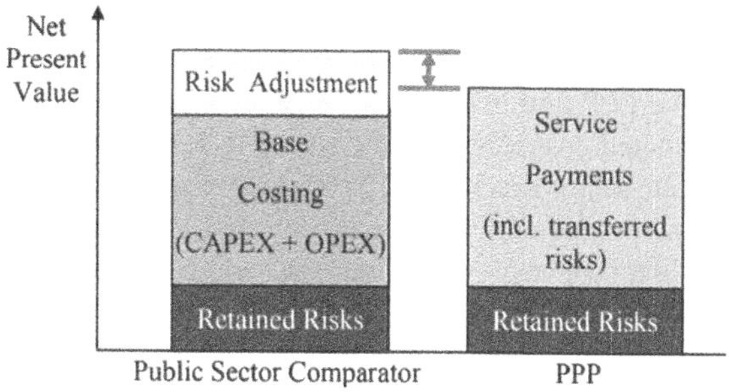

Fig. 4.4 Net present value of PSC versus PPP [2]

lower construction, operational and/or maintenance costs, time savings (through an earlier competition of the project), or quality enhancements (through enhanced service provision).

4.1.5 Public Sector Comparator (PSC)

In order to properly assess whether a PPP improves the VfM compared to traditional procurement, a Public Sector Comparator (PSC). The PSC consists in an estimate of the cost that the government would pay if it was conducting the project alone. This tool is a valuation of the lifecycle costs of the project taking into account the risks [15] and is prepared to provide a basis to assess the relevance of PPP schemes (Fig. 4.4). To provide a valid benchmark against which a PPP can be compared, the PSC must reflect not only estimated costs but also additional costs that may arise if risks materialize. PSC can also be used to assess the value of bidder´s proposals (i.e. costs, financing structure and other assumptions). The PSC can be adjusted with risk classified in two categories from a customer point of view [2]:

- **Retained risks**: They are the same within PSC and PPP.
- **Transferred risks**: They are included in the service payments but need to be taken into account in the PSC, with the risk adjustment.

In complement to risk management, the PSC estimates the hypothetical risk-adjusted cost if a project were to be financed, owned and implemented by the public sector. It is generally divided into five elements [15]:

- **Raw PSC** accounts for all lifecycle costs including public procurement costs and both capital and operating costs associated with building and maintaining the project and delivering the service over the predetermined time.
- **Financing costs** are the costs associated with arrangements to finance for a project.
- **Retained risk** refers to the value of any risk that is not transferable to the bidder.
- **Competitive neutrality** adjusts the PSC for any competitive advantages or disadvantages that accrue to a public sector.

Once the cost of a PSC is determined, the public sector typically estimates the total costs of the PPP option to the government over the life of the project. The estimate of the PPP option is defined as a shadow bid. A shadow bid is considered as "the estimated cost to the public sector if the same project were to be delivered by the private sector as a PPP" [15]. The value of payments to be made by the public sector to the private entity under shadow bid includes compensation to the private sector for lifecycle costs, financing costs and costs of risks to be transferred to the private entity, which are included within financing costs in the form of higher rates of return on debt and equity investment. A PPP may offer better value for money if the total costs calculated are less than the costs calculated by PSC or the shadow bid.

The importance for the public sector to assess the PPP option is because the transaction costs of a PPP procurement are relatively high for the public sector. Usually, the procurement process for PPP projects takes longer than traditional procurement processes. That is why PPP is only worthwhile for projects requiring a certain level of investment. For this reason, the PSC and shadow bid are developed as part of the quantitative assessment of VfM analysis conducted at the preprocurement stage. In this way, the public sector is able to assess if or not a private sector may be able to deliver the project with benefits using the bids received.

4.2 Conditions and Benefits of Public–Private Partnerships in Space Exploration

4.2.1 Potential Benefits for Public and Private Parties

PPP schemes may be pursued by public and private partners for a variety of reasons. Across the spectrum of possible structures, PPP experts identify the following list of potential benefits for public and private parties [16, see also 17 and 18]:

Potential benefits for public actors:

- **Enable the industrial sector to develop**: To promote a competitive and robust commercial space sector.
- **Rely on efficient privately managed services**: PPPs can provide an avenue for better managing the challenges using the best qualities that private sectors are offering in the space exploration market.
- **Efficiency**: Improve operation management and leverage the profit-driven efficiencies that the private sector offers in terms of schedule, costs and experience, including the state-of-the-art technology.
- **Transfer of risks and cost savings**: Operational and project execution risks are transferred from the government to the private sector which is often better able to contain costs and manage key milestones on schedule. By sharing risk between both the public and private sectors, project teams better optimized cost savings both during construction and during the project's life cycle. The cost savings were

attributed to the private sector's ability to achieve schedule certainty and cost containment throughout all phases.

- **Schedule certainty**: Under PPPs, the private sector is motivated to complete a project on time so that it can begin revenue generation.
- **Foster innovation and attract private sector capabilities**: Seek to provide better public services leveraging and collaborating with the private sector.
- **Sustainable economic growth**: Alternative risk and benefit-sharing mechanisms through an ecosystem perspective can help enable sustainable economic growth.
- **Rely on efficient privately managed services**: PPPs can provide an avenue for better managing the challenges using the best qualities that private sectors are offering in the space exploration market.
- **Value for money**: This means delivering a project with the same quality as under conventional procurement for less money, or delivering a project with superior quality for the same amount of money.

Potential benefits for private actors:

- **Return on Investment (ROI)**: In exchange for taking on public sector risk, the private sector can expect an ROI. Typically, the higher the risk, the higher the expected ROI.
- **Gain competitive advantage**: Leverage commercial technologies and intellectual property through a PPP arrangement to establish and develop the technology and gain market traction with key public sector customers.
- **Create additional revenue streams**: The private sector has the capacity to create additional revenue streams from government assets such as space-based infrastructure.
- **Implement innovations and new business**: PPPs provide greater scope for the private sector to offer innovative solutions, which can deliver the required services at a lower whole of life cost. This approach, also, helps private companies embrace innovation and bring together new financial resources and business capital to help the construction of new industry clusters, enabling innovation and new business in an increasingly competitive environment.

4.2.2 Conditions for Successful Public–Private Partnerships

A number of conditions must be met to ensure a successful PPP. In the field of space exploration, the main challenge is to find an appropriate scheme that allows both public and private partners to achieve their scientific, technical, industrial, financial and commercial objectives while remaining within acceptable boundaries.

This requires to carry out a careful evaluation of the proposed PPP, from proof of concept to implementation, to secure the complementarity and alignment of partners' objectives. Any show-stopper, i.e. a requirement of a partner (public or private) that other partners are not able or willing to meet, must be identified. Anyhow, the alignment of partners' objectives requires a high degree of flexibility to adapt project, risk and financial management practices in line with programmatic and business requirements of public and private partners.

Barriers and challenges commonly faced by PPP partners include the following technical, economic, policy, regulatory and legislative elements [16, see also 17–19]:

Political Long-term Commitments

Given the significant and long-term commitments involved, it is challenging to pursue a PPP programme without strong and stable political commitments. Political commitments need to be implemented in a proper way in order to enable an economic and efficient allocation of investments. However, a range of tools can be used to help develop and demonstrate a clear political will to develop PPPs:

- Provision by governments of incentives, subsidies, viability funding that support the development of the project and of key PPP processes, such as high-quality project preparation,
- Understanding about PPPs by politician and decision-makers with a cohesive and integrated national space strategy across government,
- Setting up and maintaining well-sourced public sector teams to assist with technically sound policy development.

Institutional Framework

To be a success, PPPs require good governance and a strong institutional framework with a well-developed administrative capacity:

- The restricted institutional capability to undertake complex and large space exploration projects at various central ministries and especially at state and local bodies´ level is obstacle to the translation of target into projects.
- The resulting institutional framework should be marched to the scope and its functions (such as project approval, policy development or technical support) and should be tailored to the gaps that have been identified.
- Necessary reporting lines, budgetary and political support and operational flexibility to effective.

Clear Regulatory Environment

PPP programmes necessitate a supportive and effective regulatory framework due to the public procurement processes involved and consistency dependence of PPPs on the use of contracts among the various parties:

- The development of PPP regulatory framework should be based on experience from existing PPP markets to avoid inappropriate restrictions on PPP project.
- Restrictions on transfer of rights in public assets to the private sector.
- Lack of coordination between national and regional governments.
- In order to attract more domestic and international funding of the infrastructure, it should need a robust regulatory environment with an independent regulator.
- Where a new PPP regulatory is required, this should be as straightforward as possible. This would allow any requirements that may be needed (usually at a later stage of PPP development) to come under administrative regulations. This

ensures that the PPP regulatory framework is more easily adaptable to changes in the PPP market. At the same time, this guarantees that the overall, more broadly defined regulatory framework approved at the national legislative level remains consistent over time and suitable for the usual needs and circumstances.

Demonstrated Technology and Capability

In general, PPPs have been effective in attracting into the market a wider range of skills, technologies and approaches from the global private sector. However, PPPs lack of flexibility to accommodate changes over the contract life and the costs sometimes associated with requesting changes to the service requirements. This may reflect poorly prepared PPP contracts, poor management of the contract, technological developments, major changes in requirement or policy or, more fundamentally, the inappropriate use of the proposed form of PPP in relation to the nature of the services. PPPs are usually best used where the long-term service requirements are predictable and stable and limited technological changes are expected.

The technology barriers can be summarized in the following three points:

- PPPs process not clearly defined,
- Non-availability of model concession agreements,
- Lack of innovations.

References

1. P. Burger, I. Hawkesworth, *How to Attain Value for Money: comparing PPP and Traditional Infrastructure Public Procurement* (2016). Retrieved from https://www.oecd.org/gov/budgeting/49070709.pdf
2. X. Bertrán, A. Vidal, *The Implementation of a Public-Private Partnership for Galileo Comparison of Galileo and Skynet 5 With Other Projects* (2005). Retrieved from http://citeseerx.ist.psu.edu/viewdoc/download?doi=10.1.1.456.4833&rep=rep1&type=pdf
3. R. Dauskardt, G. Remy, *Public Private Partnerships Frequently Asked Questions*. Retrieved from https://www.investlaos.gov.la/images/sampledata/pdf_sample/Frequently_Questions_for_PPP_Eng.pdf
4. PPP Knowledge La, *Finance Structures for PPP*. Retrieved from https://pppknowledgelab.org/guide/sections/17-finance-structures-for-ppp
5. United Nations ESCAP, *A Primer to Public-Private Partnerships in Infrastructure Development*. Retrieved from http://www.unescap.org/ttdw/ppp/ppp_primer/211_special_purpose_vehicle_spv.html
6. APMG. *Introduction to the Basic PPP Project Structure*. Retrieved from https://ppp-certification.com/ppp-certification-guide/61-introduction-basic-ppp-project-structure
7. APMG. *Defining Risk: The Risk Management Cycle*. Retrieved from https://ppp-certification.com/ppp-certification-guide/52-defining-risk-risk-management-cycle36
8. Elevate Captives. *Risk Transfer*. Retrieved from https://www.elevatecaptives.com/glossary/risk-transfer/
9. A. Blackman, *The Main Types of Business Risk* (2014). Retrieved from https://business.tutsplus.com/tutorials/the-main-types-of-business-risk--cms-22693
10. OECD Report, *Selected Good Practices For Risk Allocation And Mitigation In Infrastructure in APEC Economies* (2017). Retrieved from http://www.oecd.org/daf/fin/private-pensions/

Selected-Good-Practices-for-Risk-allocation-and-Mitigation-in-Infrastructure-in-APEC-Economies.pdf
11. P. Hovy, *Risk Allocation in Public-Private Partnerships: maximizing Value for Money* (2015). Retrieved from https://www.iisd.org/sites/default/files/publications/risk-allocation-ppp-maximizing-value-for-money-discussion-paper.pdf
12. Syracuse University, *Public-Private Partnerships, Benefits and Opportunities For Improvement within United States* (2016). Retrieved from http://eng-cs.syr.edu/wp-content/uploads/2017/04/P3Report.pdf
13. Innovative Program Delivery/US Department of Transportation, *Value for Money Assessment for Public-Private Partnerships: a Primer* (2012). Retrieved from https://www.fhwa.dot.gov/ipd/pdfs/p3/p3_value_for_money_primer_122612.pdf
14. P. Jackson, *Value for Money and International Development: Deconstructing Myths to Promote a More Constructive Discussion* (2012). Retrieved from http://www.oecd.org/development/effectiveness/49652541.pdf
15. Valuemex, *Economy, Efficiency, Effectiveness* (2012). Retrieved from http://www.en.valuemex.com/node/23
16. S.O. Babatunde, S. Perera, C. Udeaja, L. Zhou, *Identification of Barriers to Public Private Partnerships Implementation in Developing Countries.* Retrieved from http://www.irbnet.de/daten/iconda/CIB_DC27636.pdf
17. G. Martin, J. Olson, *Commercialization is Required for Sustainable Space Exploration and Development* (2009). Retrieved from https://ntrs.nasa.gov/archive/nasa/casi.ntrs.nasa.gov/20100027548.pdf
18. European Commission, *Investment Challenges in Energy, Transport and Digital Markets* (2016). Retrieved from https://ec.europa.eu/info/sites/info/files/file_import/ip041_en_2.pdf
19. K.L. Jones, *Public-Private Partnerships: stimulating Innovation In The Space Sector.* Retrieved from center for space policy and strategy (2018). http://www.aerospace.org/publications/policy-papers/public-private-partnerships-stimulating-innovation-in-the-space-sector/

Chapter 5
Towards More Ambitious Commercial Contributions to Space Exploration

5.1 Growing Opportunities for Commercial Contributions to Space Exploration

As highlighted by Mr. Gonzalez, advisor to EC director for EU Satellite Navigation Programmes, in his report on commercial space, "space commercialization results from the convergence of a bottom-up trend driven by a growing accessibility of space technology and a determined top-down policy to encourage a more market-oriented approach to space activities" [1]. Information and data compiled in this report provide clear evidence of a growing convergence between such top-down policy effort and bottom-up trend in the space exploration sector.

From a policy perspective, various objectives (i.e. optimization of programme cost-effectiveness, research of innovative concepts, support to industry development and competitiveness, contribution to economic growth) triggered a desire to foster the development of commercial space activities, including in the space exploration domain. Governments set up determined and audacious public strategies towards this goal with the underlying objectives to (1) enhance the capacity of space agencies to share risks and costs with the private industry and (2) boost innovation and market development. This ambition has been translated into new approaches to public procurement and support to research as part of an industrial policy giving more room to business considerations. The report shows that the willingness to reap benefit from a development of commercial space exploration and from a more prominent role of private industry in public programmes is a dominant consideration in the USA and Europe, the two leaders in commercial space, and provides multiple examples of new public instruments implemented on each side of the Atlantic.

From a commercial perspective, space exploration has become a domain of interest for private companies, entrepreneurs and investors, eager to engage in new, potentially rewarding, endeavours. As a result, a tangible business-driven dynamic is developing and the space exploration sector is progressively driven towards a more

C. Iacomino, *Commercial Space Exploration*,
SpringerBriefs from the European Space Policy Institute,
https://doi.org/10.1007/978-3-030-15751-7_5

commercial-oriented step. Embedded within the broader New Space context, this trend is characterized by:

- Multiple commercial endeavours from well-established players and new entrants including non-space companies and start-ups. This report proposes to organize the various models adopted by these commercial space exploration endeavours (e.g. value proposition, target market(s), cost structure, revenue streams, industrial partners) into four categories:

  - *Visionaries*: Companies targeting a very long-term and highly ambitious commercial objective in space exploration (e.g. mining of asteroids or celestial bodies, private settlements). These companies usually implement a step-wise approach based on an incremental technology development process;
  - *Exploration support service providers*: Companies offering commercial solutions that can support other private endeavours or be integrated into public exploration programmes (e.g. transportation, engineering, robotics, 3D printing, in-orbit servicing and assembly);
  - *Business opportunity seekers*: Companies leveraging opportunities created by public space exploration programmes for a commercial purpose (e.g. commercial utilization of the ISS);
  - *Autonomous exploration-related businesses*: Companies whose business model is based on solutions developed independently from public institutions and addressing mainly commercial markets (e.g. private space transportation and station for tourism or research). For these companies, public demand can be an important complement but does not constitute a pillar of business development.

  Boundaries between these categories are thin and companies may adopt multiple business profiles and/or pivot throughout their development.
- Innovative approaches to meet business requirements and commercial objectives including new concepts and methods such as industrial organization optimization, partnerships with other industries, supply chain rationalization and vertical integration, miniaturization and simplification (e.g. use of cubesats, proven technologies reuse), automation and digitization, standardized architectures or use of COTS among others. These new approaches give way to an alternative innovation dynamic where all components of innovation (i.e. technology, product, business model and process) are integrated.
- Growing private investment in commercial ventures in the space exploration domain. A consolidated assessment of global private investment in the space exploration domain has not yet been conducted, however, this report provides multiple examples of multimillion investment deals and demonstrates that space exploration has become a domain of interest for investors, eager to engage in risky yet potentially highly rewarding operations.

The growing opportunities for more significant commercial contributions to space exploration can only be the outcome of two complementary forces: a determined and long-standing effort from public actors and a favourable business dynamic in the private sector.

5.2 From "Stimulating" to "Leveraging" Commercial Contributions

The public objective to support commercial space exploration and leverage more significant private contributions (i.e. risks, costs and benefits sharing) ultimately aims to (1) improve public programmes effectiveness and efficiency and/or (2) transfer selected activities to the private sector (e.g. ISS operations) to free some budget and refocus on new missions. From this standpoint, various success stories demonstrated that more ambitious public–private partnerships can support such objectives provided that a number of conditions are met (Fig. 4.2 and Table 5.1).

Among these conditions, the capacity of the private sector to develop a profitable and sustainable business addressing, at least partially, private markets, remains a key challenge for many commercial ventures in the space exploration sector. Indeed, a vast majority of them is still at early stages of development and, even though there is confidence in the existence of business opportunities, the profitability and sustainability of the business models proposed by these companies as well as their capacity to address new sizeable private markets have yet to be demonstrated.

The public sector has an important role to play in accompaning commercial endeavours toward a fully viable stage.

From this perspective, the report shows that the combination of public policies and favourable business trends is especially instrumental in the space exploration domain where the objective to stimulate and leverage commercial solutions has become a central goal for institutions and where public support, through its various forms, (e.g. loans and subsidies, R&D funding, public demand, legal and regulatory framework adaptation) remains essential to develop a profitable and sustainable business model. Ultimately, the capacity of public actors to successfully leverage commercial contributions to space exploration and reap-associated benefits can only be the outcome of two complementary engagements:

- **On the "offer" side**, the public sector must act as a business catalyst to support the development of commercial solutions by the private industry and facilitate early business development;
- **On the "demand" side**, the public sector must act as an anchor customer to integrate commercial solutions from the private industry and support business profitability and sustainability;

The report shows that European public actors, and in particular ESA, have already made a tremendous effort on the offer side (i.e. support commercial contributions) with the introduction of new successful instruments to support commercially driven innovation (e.g. business incubation, grand challenge, investment easing) and to facilitate the emergence of new private solutions (e.g. Calls for Ideas, strategic partnerships). This effort is already yielding concrete results with several new projects and ventures having arisen in, or migrated to, Europe.

There is, however, a growing need to address, as a second step, the demand side (i.e. integrate commercial contributions) and more specifically to position public actors as

Table 5.1 Conditions and potential benefits of a successful PPP

Conditions	Potential benefits
• Maturity of partners: suitable skills and experience to manage respective responsibilities) • Improved value for money: improved economy, efficiency, effectiveness in comparison with traditional procurement) • Appropriate financial management: capacity to mitigate overprice (e.g. through open and fair competition) and budget overrun (e.g. financial management throughout the project life cycle, up to decommissioning) • Appropriate risk management: allocation of risks to the party best able to manage them and capacity of partners to manage respective risks • Adjustment of project management best practices: flexibility of partners to agree on adapted decision frameworks, shared responsibilities, project specifications, certification processes, industrial policy/set-up • Complementarity and/or alignment of partners' objectives: public programme objectives meeting business needs and vice versa • Resources availability and readiness: capacity of partners to mobilize required human, technical, financial resources • Commitment term in line with partners' requirements: PPP duration allowing partners to achieve their objectives, including return on investment • Favourable external economic and commercial conditions: capacity for private partners to achieve a profitable business case (e.g. interested customers, adequate demand) • Compliance with international and European rules and standards: compliance of the partnership with international treaties, applicable legal and regulatory regimes as well as relevant standards	**Common benefits** • Shared costs in view of meeting budget constraints or reaching the financial conditions to achieve programmatic/business objectives • Shared risks and transfer to the party best able to manage them • Shared benefits in line with respective public and private objectives as described below: **Public sector benefits** • Improved efficiency and effectiveness through incentives to achieve objectives on time and on resource • Development of industrial capabilities based on complementary public and private investment • Support for innovation and competitiveness by granting more flexibility to the private sector to pursue alternative routes (e.g. business- or process-driven innovation) • Other strategic benefits (e.g. job creation, economic growth, societal and environmental challenges) **Private sector benefits** • Additional revenues and profit (as a direct result of the PPP or through access to new revenue streams) • Competitive advantage gained as a result of a variety of positive direct or indirect PPP impacts (e.g. experience gain, new competencies, customer acquisition …) • New competencies and capabilities that can be leveraged on other verticals and markets • Technical and business innovation creating potential differentiators for industry value proposition and/or business set-up

anchor customers of commercial solutions developed by the private industry. Such anchor customer approach, which builds on the complementarity between public and private partners objectives (i.e. public programmes and business goals), seeks "to procure sufficient quantities of a commercial space product or service needed to meet government mission requirements so that a commercial venture is made viable".[1] In addition to the level of demand, the duration of the agreement also plays an essential role to provide the commercial partner with the necessary business stability to withstand temporary problems, build investors' confidence or explore new concepts or markets.

ESA has made initial steps towards a demand-driven support to commercial development with the signature of a collaboration agreement with Surrey Satellite Technology Ltd (SSTL) and Goonhilly Earth Station (GES) for Commercial Lunar Mission Support Services. Nevertheless, the facilitation of such approach does not exist in Europe yet.

The complementarity of offer- and demand-oriented initiatives is best illustrated by the recent NASA's CATALYST and Commercial Lunar Payload Services (CPLS) programmes. CATALYST encouraged and facilitated the development of US commercial robotic lunar cargo delivery capabilities (i.e. offer) and was followed up by the CLPS programme to purchase private transportation services to the lunar surface using fixed price contracts (i.e. demand). On one hand, CATALYST has been instrumental to support the emergence of various private solutions able to compete for subsequent CLPS contracts. On the other hand, it is the fixed price contracts, which integrate selected offers into NASA lunar programme that will allow the agency to actually leverage these private solutions. The two programmes are the "offer" and "demand" components serving a single public objective.

As underlined in the list of conditions for successful public–private partnerships, the integration of commercial contributions will also inevitably raise the need to adapt agencies' practices to set up adapted financial and risk management schemes, especially with commercial solutions used as critical capabilities. Indeed, if current trends progress towards a fully sustainable model—where public programmes would make steady use of commercial solutions, including for critical know-how—a situation of mutual reliance between public and private sectors would develop exposing public programmes to commercial risks. Such a situation should be properly anticipated and managed.

5.3 Way Forward

5.3.1 Commercial Potential of New Concepts

A number of promising solutions are now emerging from the cloud of commercial space exploration endeavours. Among the ventures and projects launched recently

---

[1] Title 51 of the United States Code, entitled National and Commercial Space Programs.

by the private industry, those falling in the categories of *Exploration support services providers* and *Business opportunity seekers* stand out as the most promising in their capacity to contribute to space exploration programmes (i.e. value for money, risk sharing, innovation) and meet the conditions of success mentioned above.

With regard to support services provision, various new concepts, which will be at the heart of future space exploration programmes, offer an interesting potential to develop a more demand-driven approach to public–private partnerships based on (1) repeatable standard service purchase, (2) complementarity of public and private objectives, (3) development of market opportunities, and (4) fair industry competition. These promising support service concepts include, among others:

- In-orbit operations, manufacturing and assembly,
- In Situ Resource Utilization (including resource exploration, mining and processing),
- Station and base operations,
- Transportation and payload hosting.

As pointed out previously, the implementation of more ambitious public–private partnerships for the development and provision of these new services will require agencies to adapt their approach including industrial policy and procurement rules. The key challenge for agencies will find the right balance between the willingness to exercise top-down control over the development and distribution of space capabilities and the necessary loosening of this control to meet business requirements.

5.3.2 The Role of Private Actors in the Post-ISS Era

The considerations mentioned above are expected to take on their full meaning in the post-ISS era. In particular, Lunar Gateway plans will require a great deal of transportation and in-orbit/in situ operations and assembly which will provide fruitful ground for the delivery of services by the private industry. To prepare for such an era of space exploration and human spaceflight programmes building more extensively and prominently on partnerships between public and private actors, the ISS provides an essential test bed.

The private sector has been expected to develop business cases for the utilization of the ISS since the inception of the programme. This old promise materialized only partially and commercial activities remained, first and foremost, valuable complementary contributions. Nevertheless, with the declared objective to transfer ISS operations to the private industry and end direct funding to the programme by 2025 to free budget for the Lunar Gateway, the current US administration seems confident that, in the current ecosystem, the station has the potential to fulfil this long-awaited goal.

The US administration contemplates a two-step approach on the offer and demand model described previously:

- First, to stimulate the emergence of an offer by 2025 and facilitate business development, the US Budget allocates \$150 million "to encourage the development of capabilities that the private sector and NASA can use"[2];
- Then, to leverage the complementarity between public and private objectives (i.e. cost savings for the public sector and business profitability and sustainability for the private industry), NASA would become a customer of solutions offered by the station for its low Earth orbit research and technology demonstration requirements.

Beyond the objective to phase out of the programme to refocus on the Moon, a progressive transfer of ISS operations to the private sector would also pave the way towards public–private partnerships for the post-ISS era and, in particular, the Lunar Gateway programme that is planned to integrate more ambitious partnerships with the private industry. The proposal to transfer the ISS to the private sector is audacious and will likely face multiple political, diplomatic, legal, technical, industrial, operational and commercial challenges. Notwithstanding, this proposal allows to project the challenges ahead of space agencies on the difficult road towards more significant commercial contributions to space exploration.

NASA is consulting with their national space industry on a potential transfer of the ISS operations, but international partners are not formally involved in this process. Notwithstanding, a unilateral decision from the US to end direct federal support to the ISS in 2025 and to adopt such commercial approach would have a considerable impact on the operations of partners' modules, including in terms of accessibility. This scenario would require in-depth investigations from international partners, including Europe, to consider the range of options at hand to conciliate their respective objectives, interests and financial capacities in such a new context. Beyond these issues, this scenario would also require to discuss the conditions for European industry to participate, through competition or industry-to-industry cooperation frameworks, to a commercialization of the station either as a partner for commercial operations or as a customer/user of the station. Such discussion, which should account for existing and upcoming partnerships with the European private sector for the ISS exploitation, should be supported by a consultation to assess industry's interest and by an examination of the conditions to be met for European participation including the need to set up appropriate arrangements with the USA. A policy in this sense should also anticipate necessary activities (e.g. R&D, demonstration, qualification …) to support the emergence of European champions.

Reference

1. A. González, *A Snapshot of Commercial Space*. CSTPR white Paper (2017). Retrieved from http://sciencepolicy.colorado.edu/admin/publication_files/white_papers/2017.01.pdf

---

[2]Budget of the U.S. Government, Fiscal Year 2019.

The manufacturer's authorised representative in the EU is Springer Nature Customer Service Centre GmbH, Europaplatz 3, 69115 Heidelberg, Germany. If you have any concerns regarding our products, please contact ProductSafety@springernature.com

Printed and bound by CPI Group (UK) Ltd, Croydon, CR0 4YY
30/09/2026
02225258-0005